"In *Ghana to the World*, chef Eric Adjepong defines culinary sankofa, presenting traditional recipes as well as his new Ghanaian American creations that are destined to become contemporary classics. The recipes are interspersed with family stories and accompanied by glorious photographs. This is a book to savor, to cook from, to read, to gift, and, most importantly, to keep."

–JESSICA B. HARRIS, PhD,
culinary historian, lecturer, author, and professor emeritus

"This book is nothing short of a love letter to Ghana and an homage to its cuisine. Thank you, Chef Eric, for blessing us with this deep-dive immersion into the rich diversity of Ghanaian cuisine."

–PIERRE THIAM,
James Beard Award–winning chef and cookbook author

"I'm so excited to start cooking from Eric's book, *Ghana to World*. West African cooking, especially Ghanaian, has a special place in my heart. He works to push boundaries and show how African cuisines are important to global food culture. I look forward to being able to cook these incredible recipes at home for and with my family."

–MARCUS SAMUELSSON,
award-winning chef and author

"*Ghana to the World* is much more than a collection of recipes connecting Eric's family's past, present, and dreams for the future. It's a proclamation of just how integral and undeniable West African cuisine is to modern American cooking. Loaded with stunning imagery and mouth-watering recipes that transport you between continents, *Ghana to the World* is a vibrant celebration of a chef at his peak!"

–GAIL SIMMONS,
food expert, TV host and author of *Bringing It Home*

"Eric has always honored the food of the African diaspora in his cooking. I've been lucky to try it firsthand myself. Through the recipes in *Ghana to the World*, you are now given the opportunity to share in this rich and delicious cultural exploration."

–TOM COLICCHIO,
chef and owner of Crafted Hospitality

"By exploring his West African lineage, Eric honors food history and propels forward an important dialogue about African cooking at the same time. Chefs often use their own story to articulate how they found cooking in the first place; Eric poetically shares his story through these recipes, and I can't wait to cook and learn from this book!"

–ALEX GUARNASCHELLI,
chef, cookbook author, and TV host

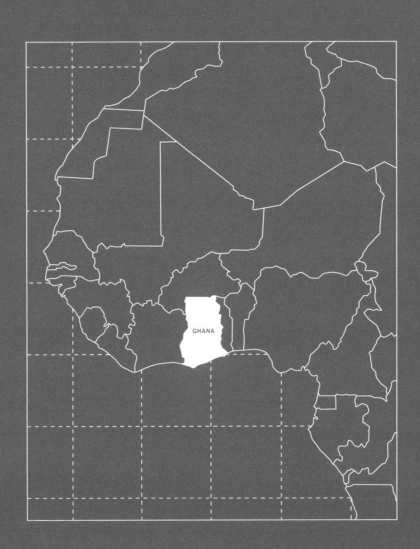

GHANA

GHANA TO THE WORLD

GHANA
TO THE
WORLD

Recipes and Stories That Look Forward
While Honoring the Past

ERIC ADJEPONG

with Korsha Wilson

Photographs by Doaa Elkady and Carlos Idun-Tawiah

CLARKSON POTTER/PUBLISHERS
NEW YORK

To my late father, Benjamin Adjepong.
Thank you, Dad.

Contents

Foreword
by Chef Alexander Smalls

I was watching TV one Saturday morning at home in my Harlem apartment and while surfing the channels, I happened to randomly discover a show where a Black chef was being interviewed about his career. He spoke about growing up in both the Bronx and Accra, studying in London, and his then recent move to Washington, D.C. I was fascinated by the passion of his words and the clarity of his resolve, by the discipline and focus he displayed. I was also moved by the familiar stories of how valued life experiences came out of the foodways that are shared with family and community. It was not just his story but mine as well. It wasn't until the end of the broadcast that his full name made the credits… "Eric Adjepong"… never to be forgotten.

Over the years, Eric and I would run into each other at various events, restaurants, and festivals. He had really grown as a chef—cutting his chops in a number of quality kitchens and building his reputation to make a name for himself as a chef. He was beginning to catch fire.

Eric Adjepong is a culinary poet (maybe a prophet, if not a magician) who is on a mission to excite flavor and express heritage in every dish he creates and prepares for the world, like so many of us who choose or are chosen by the need to be a part of this demanding age-old discipline. The profession of cooking seemed a fitting choice for his creativity and talents. Eric's wealth of experiences that came from growing up in two worlds—West Africa and America—provided a rich cultural foundation as he explored not only where he came from but who he is.

He found his identity in these dual environments separated by a vast ocean of languages, traditions, different foods, and racial strife. Cooking became his go-to; a way to find value and worth, while making himself and others happy.

In Eric's world, food and the engagement of eating became a reservoir, a container for his emotional wellbeing, and a collection of positive feelings, happy memories of relatives, the good times of his childhood, and loved ones. Food memories became something that could keep and protect his spirit, which made him feel whole and safe as a boy who would become a remarkable man. He would ultimately find his own voice and establish his talents while coming to terms with challenging circumstances, and navigating his way in an ever-changing reality cooking landscape would be his salvation.

So it was no surprise to me when I landed in Macau, China, to judge the final round of Bravo's *Top Chef* that I would run into Chef Eric. I was the first person he ran into outside of the set after being eliminated from the competition. I had no idea the pressure and the momentum that would collapse in our embrace as he teared up and quietly whispered into my ear, "I tried to hold on chef, I tried to wait for you . . ." And with that it became clear to me just how important this meal was not only to Eric and his career but to Black people, particularly African people using food to bridge the cultural gaps of identity and acceptance. For Eric, his cooking was (and still is) uniting the two worlds he has always lived in . . . Africa and America.

I was touched and unsettled knowing the enormous weight that Eric was carrying squarely on his shoulders for the wealth of all of us. A meal that was intended to heal and validate a mission, a purpose, a reckoning of history, and a heritage. Nothing seemed more important to me. It was beyond crushing when I learned he had been eliminated, especially given the final results of the show.

This cookbook is Eric's story: it's what he has been preparing himself to give us his entire life. It is his way of setting the table, offering a gift, healing the wounds of the world, and making a better world for his little girl.

I was honored to accompany him and Korsha Wilson on their trip to Ghana in preparation for the writing of this book. *Ghana to the World* is the perfect accompaniment for Eric's engaging culinary contributions and for the advancement of the food of the African diaspora. He is an important voice and practitioner in the culinary field, and his work helps to unravel the grip of six hundred years of institutional racism and unfair practices in the culinary profession. He found his voice through the cultural narrative and lens of our heritage, life's unapologetic circumstances, through pain, joy, disappointments, and shortcomings. Through it all, Eric invites us to sit, dine from his table, and enjoy the conversation and the brilliant flavors of his life on a plate.

In your hands is a world he has created for all of us to feel the lyrical engagement of his life and for that reason, my friend, it is my pleasure to accept your invitation.

Thanks for serving up this amazing feast.

Introduction

One of the questions I get asked the most by people I'm meeting for the first time is "How'd you get into this?" It could be at a food event, or in an interview, or just in casual conversation. They want to know about my path to becoming a chef and how I knew I wanted to pursue this career. Looking back, becoming a chef feels like it was destined—a logical gathering of many threads in my story.

Food has always been at the center of my life, helping me understand myself and my place in the world. There were comforting West African stews in my childhood house in Yonkers, New York; the classical French dishes from my time in culinary school in Providence, Rhode Island; those golden-brown bofrot I ate outside of my grandparents' house in Kumasi, Ghana—each experience holds an important place informing my love of food and how I see my love of food, my perspective, and the act of cooking.

> *Being both West African and American ties me to the continent, to America, and to the generations-long story of people with similar skin tones to mine whose ancestors made the journey so many hundreds of years ago.*

From a young age, seeing my mother cook and watching chefs on TV showed me that I could use this skill and change a bunch of ingredients into a dish that could evoke emotion in whoever was eating it. The process used to cook humble ingredients could not only morph those products into anything, it could also make a viewer or someone nearby feel something. That intrigued me and fascinated me. It still does. I had some support: my guidance counselor in high school pointed me toward culinary arts as a way to embrace my love of science and also as a way to show my personality. And my mom encouraged me to go to school for it. I didn't know it then, but cooking would become my outlet for showing instead of telling others about my background, my family, and how I see the world.

I've been thinking about telling this story for a long time. About how being a first-generation Ghanaian American shapes how I see things, and how my story is similar to many immigrant family stories yet also unique because of my place in the world and the time that I'm alive. The foods that I eat and encounter as I travel help me draw connections and see the differences between cultures. Being both West African and American ties me to the continent, to America, and to the generations-long story of people with similar skin tones to mine whose ancestors made the journey so many hundreds of years ago.

I've used food to talk about these connections in restaurants and on television, but writing it out, looking at it as one cohesive story and as a picture that's still being painted, has required me to look both forward and backward in time in order to understand how I got here and where I want to go. It was clear to me that there was a fluidity between these past and present moments. So over the course of writing this book, one thing became clear: my story is sankofa, a Ghanaian adinkra symbol depicted by an image of a backward-facing bird flying forward, carrying an egg in its mouth. Whether you're in Accra, Kumasi, or on the coast, you'll see it in paintings on street corners or as metal artwork—it's omnipresent as a guiding principle. Adinkra symbols—simple line drawings that create a set of West African iconography—tell stories and represent core life lessons. In Twi, sankofa reads as "Se wo were fi na wosan kofa a yenki," which translates to "It is not taboo to go back and fetch what you forgot."

The sankofa symbol has become a foundational belief and mission for many African Americans and Black chefs, telling us that sometimes, in order to move forward, we have to look backward. For me, it's a beautiful, prescient reminder that we must understand where we came from to see who we are and where we need to go. A life of traveling back and forth between America and Ghana has shown me how much each place informs my work as a chef and my identity. Much like sankofa, I work to carry the gift of calling both West Africa and America home into all that I do.

This book is a reflection of the journey I undertook to understand the many parts of my identity and the wisdom that those places, tastes, and memories hold for me. Writing these recipes and this story has enabled me to express and celebrate my life through food while also looking at the trials I've faced and the triumphs I've achieved. But, as with anything, I can create only through my own lens, showing my point of view. Interpretation is tricky, since it requires seeing the inspiration and staying true to it while adding elements that enhance without masking the brilliance of the original. I don't represent all Ghanaians or Ghanaian Americans, just me, and I'm working with classic dishes and different techniques to make food that represents me and my perspective. The recipes here are dishes you can enjoy, but they're also stories about how I got creative with the food I grew up with and incorporated things I've seen, learned, and tasted throughout my journey, balancing the traditional and the modern, making dishes that are true to their essence while also reflecting my own story as a Ghanaian American.

Cooking is a creative, occasionally frustrating, and rewarding practice that helps me express myself. It allows me to not only transport myself to different places, but take people along, bringing them into my world and how I see things. That means a lot to me—to be able to help someone experience a little bit of what life is like outside of their purview feels like a superpower. It's my favorite part of being a chef.

Much like sankofa, I work to carry the gift of calling both West Africa and America home into all that I do.

I wrote this book to push the boundaries of what many people think Africa is and isn't. I feel a responsibility as a chef to bring tradition and culture to my cooking but also to think about the lineage of West African cooking, to create a cohesive message of how impactful Africa as a continent and West Africa as a region are to food culture globally. And that by looking to the continent we can look at the past and the future. This book continues that legacy. What's exciting is that it's only the beginning. I'm still evolving and understanding the world. Even though I have a very strong sense of who I am, the world around me is still moving and changing, and I continue to grow. You'll see how my path to becoming a chef unfolded and how by looking back, I was able to move forward, and I hope you see how sankofa can be applied to your life too.

Sankofa
A Way of Living and Cooking

"We face neither East nor West: we face forward."

—Kwame Nkrumah, during a speech in
Accra, Ghana, on April 7, 1960

Makola Market, the largest open-air market in Ghana's capital city, Accra, sounds chaotic. The market is seemingly endless and high-energy from the movement of crowds of people talking, bartering, and exchanging products among a continuous symphony of horns honking in nearby traffic. Here produce and goods from all over the African continent are for sale: vibrant green okra standing in woven baskets, brownish-yellow plantains soft and ready to be fried, green shelled coconuts stacked hip high on tables. Shiny dried copper-red shrimp are stacked in bowls, and fresh fish caught in the Atlantic that morning, still wet, are displayed on wooden slabs in front of women waiting to scale and gut them for buyers.

Each area of Makola Market has a unique scent: the preserved meats section has a good funk to it, like a dry-aged steak, from air-exposed fat and meat dehydrating over many days. The cosmetics section is fragrant with warm shea butter and essential oils. Even the fabrics for sale give off their aromas, as the humidity in the air lifts the smell of wax and cotton from spools of brightly colored wax-print fabric and clothes. Your nose could also guide you to the spice section of the market, where overfilled tin canisters piled high with fragrant spices form triangular points of various colors, like small pyramids.

In every corner and every walkway, there are people shopping, sightseeing, or selling something. Hundreds, if not thousands, of people move fluidly between vendors, between cars, and between each other at a fast pace, while buses display sun-bleached red, green, and yellow paint. Traffic is often at a standstill, yet people are still honking, and on the buses, people hang out of the windows, banging on the sides. Every color you can think of is present in the fabrics for sale and on the bodies moving around you, the hues heightened by the sun overhead that feels like it turns up the contrast on everything.

Even though there's a lot going on, each time I've walked through Makola Market over the years, it has felt familiar and enticing to me, engaging all of my senses. As a chef, I love seeing, smelling, and tasting what's available to cook with, and as a Ghanaian, I love being in a place where people look like me, my mom, my aunts, my uncles. Surrounded by fellow Ghanaians, I feel a deep ease and sense of belonging. I feel like I'm home.

But while I might fit in at first glance, my American accent gives me away when I start speaking Twi, a language spoken in Ghana and many West African countries, making it clear that home is also somewhere else for me.

New York City is where I was born and raised. I'm just as comfortable in a subway station in the Bronx as I am in Makola Market. Walking around in Manhattan puts me at ease in a different way. Not in the sense that everyone shares a similar skin tone as me like in Ghana, but in that I've spent much of my life here: whether it was driving by Madison Square Garden with my dad in his taxi or heading to a restaurant in Tribeca for shifts when I was a line cook.

I was born in Manhattan and visited Ghana for the first time when I was two years old. The story is that my father and mother wanted to get married but that first he needed his family's approval, so he took me to Kumasi, the cultural capital of Ghana, where both of my parents are from, to show his mother how serious this relationship had become. I was essentially living proof, a token of their love for one another and their hopes to build a family together. The approval he was seeking never materialized because my grandmother had someone else in mind for my father to marry and wasn't too happy when he told her about my mom. We stayed in Ghana for a couple more weeks visiting more family, but my parents ended up breaking up not long after that trip, and my mother eventually married my stepfather, Mr. John Bophar Abeberese, who is also from Kumasi. I wouldn't see my father again until years later.

After that trip, my mother and father went back to work in the United States, but left me with my mother's parents in Kumasi for about three years. It was just the three of us, me and my grandparents, spending time together. Even though I was very young, memories of that time come to me like flashes of lightning: playing in their front yard and running around a huge tree in the afternoons, or riding around their house in a toy police car I loved. My time there made an impression on my taste buds and my sense of where I come from.

The stories from my grandparents, aunts, and uncles describing that period I spent in Kumasi as a child center mostly around the local street vendors who walked along the streets selling stews, skewers of grilled meat, and warm bofrot. According to my grandparents, I would yell out "Kotonbre! Kotonbre!" (my favorite spinach stew) and "Bofrot! Bofrot!" to the vendors whenever I saw them, like a kid in the United States chasing an ice cream truck. They thought it was funny. To this day, those things I enjoyed during my first trip to Ghana are still some of my favorite things to eat.

After I moved back to New York City, bofrot continued to be one of my favorite dishes that reminded me of my time in Kumasi with my grandparents. If you've never had bofrot, it's a fried sweet yeasted doughnut with hints of nutmeg. (To give it some extra love, I like to roll it in some cinnamon sugar.) The deep-fried balls of dough were served at every get-together our West African community had. I remember seeing aunties frying bofrot and handing the hot, pillowy, dark caramel–colored pieces to us kids to eat while they were still warm. Now that I'm older and have traveled a bit, I realize that this way of nurturing through taste buds happens on both sides of the Atlantic.

Ghana and America may seem vastly different, but they share similarities through food. I was too young to notice these parallels as a child, but as I grew up, I started to see how I was connected to both Ghana and America, both places inextricably tied to who I am and my upbringing.

The common thread of all of it is the movement of people of African descent, either involuntarily or voluntarily, to different parts of the world. The transatlantic slave trade in particular has had a lasting impact on the United States, creating the foundation for most of what we consider to be American cuisine. In an essay about enslaved Africans' impact on Brazilian cuisine, historian Dr. Scott Alves Barton wrote that Africans brought to the Americas were "empty handed but not empty headed." This truth can be seen in so many of what we consider to be American regional foods: bofrot is a cousin to the beignet of New Orleans. Jambalaya is a derivative of jollof. The magenta-colored drink called sobolo, sorrel, or zobo is a familiar sight all over the diaspora and a close cousin to red drink in America.

The forced migration of Africans impacted the cuisine of every single country that enslaved Africans were brought to, and as the transatlantic slave trade spread to the Caribbean, the American South, and South America, ingredients and cooking techniques traveled too, blending cultures and cuisines to create something unique with strong foundational ties to Africa. Exploring those ties in my cooking and drawing on their similarities and contrasts is my way of honoring them. In doing so, I'm teaching diners about those connections too, and ensuring proper credit is given to the people who were forced to endure that transatlantic journey and their descendants on both sides. Through my pop-up dinners I've been able to cook for people all over the world, and one of the things I hear most often from fellow Africans and African Americans is how familiar the flavors taste despite the difference in presentation. Acknowledging those shared flavors, cooking techniques, and dishes will help us move forward while recognizing where we've come from—this is the heart of sankofa.

At this current moment in my life, I try to face the present while keeping an eye to the flavors and dishes that impacted me the most. I think about how I can use different techniques to make these dishes my own, paying homage to the past and looking toward the future. The push-pull of tradition and modernity are a part of my cooking, and I work to balance them, never losing sight of the flavors and dishes that speak to my West African heritage while also addressing the current moment.

That's how things continue to move forward. In my house, making bofrot brings up memories of that first trip to Ghana decades ago. That taste has stayed with me, and I'm now able to pass this dish on to my daughter, handing her warm, pillowy bofrot just like the aunties in my community did for me when I was a kid. When I make them, I see how much my daughter enjoys them and how we're creating memories too.

For me, sankofa is powerful because it contains so many lessons. Sankofa requires patience and grace. Patience because time is the greatest teacher of all, and grace because mistakes will be made and you have to forgive yourself for making them. It's also about giving back to the community you came from. But in order to do that, you have to first help yourself and be sure of who you are and where you come from, before you can give others a leg up. You can't pour from an empty cup; to have a full cup means you're whole, willing to give freely of what's overflowing from the top.

Looking back to the past, to the ancestors, for lessons for the future feels like it's woven into the fabric of Ghana; the people, the culture, all of it points back to one another. The place and the soil are absolutely the source of how I approach my work as a chef, from the stories I want to tell, to the techniques I use, to the way the ingredients interact on the plate. When I cook, I use smoke, salt, earthiness, and char as baseline flavors because those tastes show up in Ghana's cuisine again and again, in dishes like grilled chichinga (page 229), which is the ultimate street food; the savory-sweet Tom Brown breakfast porridge (page 51); and earthy, rich groundnut soup (page 103).

Both America and Ghana shape how I see the world and my place in it, and definitely how I experience life in both places. Being African and American in equal measure provides me with two places to physically rest my head and two places in which I can anchor my heart. I know wherever I go in the world, I can always return to Ghana or America to visit my family and see not only where I've been but where I'm going. That's the spirit of sankofa in action.

How to Use This Book

If you're hoping to be able to open this book and get a quick overview of West Africa, this isn't the cookbook for you, because it is not a guide to traditional West African cuisine. Full stop. Instead, this cookbook is a mixture of both traditional and updated West African recipes. Traditional dishes like Kontomire Abomu (page 158), Waakye Stew (page 95), and Fufu (page 176) follow the techniques that I learned from my mother and aunties, similar to how many West African families cook now and have cooked for generations. The more modern interpretations blend traditional Ghanaian recipes, ingredients, and techniques—my baseline—with those from other cultures I've encountered through travels or while cooking in professional restaurant kitchens. These dishes speak to my life now, like fried chicken with berbere glaze (page 209), Sticky Tamarind-Glazed Duck Legs (page 218), and fried rice flavored with earthy miso made from benne seeds (page 201). It's important to me to show how dynamic West African dishes, ingredients, and techniques can be, so the recipes here reflect that. I also wanted to keep you, the modern home cook, in mind, and update certain techniques to match the tools that may be available in your home kitchen.

 On recipes that are traditional versions of classic dishes, you'll find a sankofa symbol, indicating that I'm looking back to dishes that informed my upbringing, rooted in West African cooking, and sharing them with you.

 More updated versions of dishes will have another symbol, nea onnim, a symbol of knowledge, lifelong education, and a continued quest for understanding. These recipes speak to how I combine flavors and ingredients that excite me.

The whole recipe list is a blend of many parts of my life, coming together to create my style of cooking. I hope that this cookbook encourages you to get familiar with these dishes and the ingredients used, or helps you see them another way if you already know them. I also hope it pushes you to look at how you combine all the parts of yourself and your identity in your cooking.

My Sankofa Toolkit

My sankofa cooking style—melding the different influences in my life, looking back to move forward—starts here, with the ingredients and tools that show up in my cooking over and over again. Some of these ingredients, like groundnuts and their close relative, peanuts, are a big component in both West African and American cooking, pointing to the ways in which African ingredients and influence are on both sides of the Atlantic. Others, like crayfish powder, show up in West African households and enclaves all over the world, connecting the African continent to points around the globe.

PANTRY INGREDIENTS

Benne Seeds and Benne Miso

These ivory-colored seeds come from Benin, near Ghana. Used just like sesame, benne seeds are an ingredient that I think deserves way more acknowledgment because of all of the attributes they bring to the dishes they're incorporated into, offering a nutty aroma and taste, with crunch and textural contrast. I like Anson Mills' benne seeds from the Sea Islands of South Carolina. You can use them in both savory and sweet applications. One of my favorite ways to use them is to toast them and blend them into a benne miso paste that resembles the flavor and texture of tahini. Keepwell Vinegar is my favorite brand of benne miso, which is toasty and nuttier than your typical miso paste, but red or brown miso paste will do in a pinch.

Calabash Nutmeg

Calabash nutmeg, or African nutmeg, is indigenous to Africa and grows there with big sunburst-colored petals. It's similar to the spice you may already be familiar with but has an added earthy flavor similar to black pepper.

To use it, you have to toast the whole shell and then crack it, usually in a mortar and pestle, to expose the pod. The spicy bite of calabash can often be found in bofrot recipes and pepper soup and stews, where it adds a spiced base that is hard to distinguish but is missed when it's not there. I love adding it to spice mixes so it can lend its flavor while working in harmony with other ingredients.

Chef Zoe Adjonyoh sells it online in her marketplace at ZoesGhanaKitchen.com.

Crayfish Powder (or Shrimp Powder)

In markets across West Africa, you'll find containers piled with whole dried little shrimp, used to make an important foundational flavor of many dishes: African crayfish powder. Nigerians use this ingredient a lot more than Ghanaians, but we both use it to make shito, the condiment you'll find throughout both countries. It's our version of fish sauce but in dry form, offering a jolt of savory, funky, umami flavor and a fermented backbone to anything it's added to.

You can find it at African supermarkets as powder (crayfish and shrimp powders can be used interchangeably), but I recommend buying the dried shrimp whole and using a spice grinder to blend them to a texture and consistency you like. At home I give my dried shrimp a couple of quick pulses in the food processor to create a chunky grind that is not completely fine, so it adds texture to my dishes.

Egusi Seeds

Egusi seeds come from the egusi gourd, indigenous to West Africa. You'd be forgiven for thinking the striped light green melon is similar to a watermelon in terms of taste, but the egusi melon is very different. For one, it's bitter instead of sweet, and its seeds are the real prize. The flat white oval-shaped seeds are harvested from the sun-dried flesh of egusi melons and are packed with nutrients, proteins, and oils. Commonly consumed in Ghana, Nigeria, and Cameroon, egusi seeds are known for their distinctively nutty flavor, which makes them a versatile ingredient for both savory and sweet recipes. They can be found online or in African markets and you can buy them whole or ground into a powder and use them in soups, stews, or porridges. My favorite brand is Jeb Foods.

Fonio

Fonio is an ancient grain produced in West Africa that is technically the small seeds of a type of grass found and cultivated in the region. The grain is high in vitamin B, iron, zinc, and magnesium yet was still relatively unknown in the West until 2017, when chef (and my friend) Pierre Thiam began heralding fonio as an easy-to-cook alternative to well-known grains like quinoa and millet. You can find it at Whole Foods as well as online at Chef Thiam's website, Yolele.com.

Garden Egg

You'll see these orb-like pale yellow and white eggplants on market tables everywhere in West Africa. They're a humble ingredient that's a key component in garden egg stew and light soup (page 108). They have an intense earthy flavor and are very filling. Seeing merchants selling slices of grilled garden egg with salt is common in Ghana because this vegetable grows in such abundance.

To be honest, it's not my favorite ingredient, but I understand its importance in West African cooking, and it's a big part of everyone's diet there. There are two recipes that call for garden egg in this book. Look for garden eggs at your local African market

sold fresh, frozen, or brined in cans. If you can't find garden egg, then you can use a Japanese eggplant.

Gari

Cassava is a star ingredient and commodity in the diets of so many African descendants. Gari (or garri) is granulated flour made from the cassava root. The cassava is peeled, grated, then pressed to extract the liquid from the pulp. That pulp is sifted and fermented for several days and then roasted until it becomes dry and crispy. The resulting powder, gari, is a shelf-stable product that can be used in baking, made into cereals, and rehydrated into swallows. You can find it online or at any African market or grocery store.

Grains of Selim

Also known as Senegal pepper or negro pepper, this black pepper–like spice is native to Africa and adds a complex background flavor to stews, soups, and even drinks, such as Sobolo (page 89). Its uniquely spicy undertone and floral quality adds more depth than black pepper. I especially love it in place of pepper in spice mixes and seasoning rubs like the Suya Spice Blend (page 35). Grains of Selim can be easily found online at chef Zoe Adjonyoh's website, ZoesGhanaKitchen.com, or at your local African market.

Groundnuts

Although peanuts are originally from South America, they were planted across the southern United States by enslaved West Africans who were familiar with the groundnut, a similar species. In fact, the word *goober*, which peanuts are sometimes called, is actually from the Congolese *nguba*. The sheen on a groundnut is something that's really beautiful to me, matched only by the earthy, nutty smell of freshly roasted groundnuts. In Ghana, they're much smaller than the variety that grows in the States, and they're also more intensely flavorful than American peanuts.

In Ghana, groundnuts are not only snacks but also a key ingredient in soups and stews, lending their nutty flavor and awesome texture to whatever they're added to. Like peanuts, their natural form offers crunch and earthiness, and when pureed, they add a pleasing silkiness to the palate. In America, you can find peanuts in all sorts of foods, from a peanut butter and jelly sandwich that is the quintessential kid food, to peanut brittle as a traditional treat, to the always popular peanut M&Ms.

Like plantains (see page 31), groundnuts came from somewhere else and have become an immovable part of West African cuisine.

An assortment of important ingredients from across the diaspora: Scotch bonnets, jalapeños, piri piri peppers, black-eyed peas, and benne seeds.

When I was growing up, my mom's asanka (see page 32) was a common sight, and I'd watch as she rhythmically mashed ingredients like ginger, tomatoes, and garlic in the grooved bowl.

Some of the most common ingredients you'll see across the African diaspora: green okra pods, sturdy plantains, and yuca or cassava root.

In this book you'll see groundnuts and peanuts utilized for both their texture and complex flavor. If you can get groundnuts, please do—their flavor is richer, with more depth than the peanuts we get in the States. They're available online, but if you can't find them, just go ahead and use the peanuts called for in the recipes, which have a more versatile flavor. They become a salsa of sorts on top of the Pan-Seared Grouper with Fried Peanut Salsa on page 186, and they're the basis for the soup with guinea fowl on page 103.

Maggi Seasoning Cubes

Maggi seasoning cubes are a popular food seasoning product that is widely used in West Africa, including Ghana. Maggi is a brand owned by the food and beverage company Nestlé, whose products were introduced to the region during the late 1950s. Maggi quickly became an integral part of local cooking traditions, especially during the age of industrialization when Ghanaians searched for more work outside of their homes. When you see Maggi cubes in a recipe in this book, I'm referring to the commonly used Nestlé brand, which is readily available online and at most grocery stores as well as your local African market.

Okra

There's a love-hate relationship with this ingredient around the world, but there's no denying the importance of okra and how distinctive it is. Okra isn't a background ingredient; it shows up with its texture and color and makes its presence known.

The origins are disputed, but the most common story is that it was introduced to the Moors in thirteenth-century Egypt or Ethiopia. From there, the seeds were brought to other parts of the continent and to the New World during the transatlantic slave trade in the sixteenth century.

There are so many ways to eat okra: fried, grilled, stewed. It's a super versatile ingredient. I think people are intimidated by it, but once you learn how to buy it and cook it, you'll feel more confident. When you're buying okra, look for vibrant green pods that are blemish-free. When you pick one up, it should have heft to it and not feel hollow. Local is always best, but if you don't have access to fresh okra, you can definitely use frozen.

Piri Piri

It's hard to think of a time when this chili wasn't part of African cooking, especially since it's also called African bird's-eye chili, but this bright red chili pepper has traveled the world. Originally derived from plants in the Americas, this pepper, also known as peri peri or pili pili, was brought to Africa by the Portuguese during their colonization of eastern Africa. In fact, the Swahili word for "pepper" is *pilipili*. It has since made its way to western Africa and Ghana, where it became a big part of the cooking. It's very spicy (about ten times hotter than a jalapeño) but also has sweet and floral notes. You can buy it dried and rehydrate it to make sauces. It's used a lot in spice blends to flavor kebabs or grilled meat and can also be used as a marinade. Piri piri sauce is the special sauce at Nando's, an international restaurant chain serving Mozambique-style grilled spicy chicken. I love that sauce.

Recently it's become pretty easy to buy via online grocery stores. Chef Zoe Adjonyoh sells it in her marketplace at ZoesGhanaKitchen.com.

Plantains

Plantains take on so many forms as they cross borders into different dishes. An important ingredient in Ghana, plantains are also prevalent on every Caribbean island, in every Latin country, and in every part of West Africa I've been to, in varying textures: fried in thick slices or in chips, mashed, baked, roasted. This fruit is well represented on dinner tables, as snacks, and as an ingredient in iconic dishes such as kelewele. It's used in every stage of ripeness: green and starchy, slightly sweet and yellow with black spots, and completely black, as sweet as it'll ever be. The versatility of plantains is unmatched.

Unfortunately, the history of the plantain and how it came to West Africa isn't well documented, but it's believed the plantain originated in Southeast Asia and was traded between the Bantu peoples. Plantains acted as currency, which helped them expand their influence westward over the continent, and this influence is still felt: Ghana is the world's second-largest producer.

In this book both the Kelewele (page 75) and the Sweet Fried Plantains (page 157) are a good jumping-off point for exploring this ingredient. I encourage you to buy some plantains in their green stage and some that are yellow with dark spots and cook with both so you can experience the differences in flavors and textures that are possible.

Prekese

Prekese isn't used often in this book, but I'd be remiss if I didn't mention it here. In West Africa, prekese is a medicinal plant used as an anti-inflammatory and for digestive and immune health. These elongated dark brown pods hang from the Aidan tree and are primarily used in cooking to fragrance and flavor soups, stews, and drinks. The flavor is pronounced, slightly sweet, and tangy. The pods have a bark-like texture with pulp and seeds on the inside, which makes it easy to incorporate into many dishes by crushing or chopping, or by slow extraction via a low-heat cooking method. You can find prekese online at retailers like Amazon and Walmart. My favorite brand is Herb to Body.

Salt (Diamond Crystal Kosher)

One of my favorite quotes about salt comes from chef David Viana, an amazing cook and friend whom I was lucky enough to compete against in *Top Chef 16*. Chef David says that you have to date, then be monogamous with, your salt. Since culinary school, I've been married to Diamond Crystal kosher salt. It isn't traditional, as the salt used in Ghana is typically iodized table salt, but for me, the size of the crystals and the flavor of the salt are the best. And the industry agrees, since it's the most common salt chefs use.

TOOLS

Asanka

This earthenware bowl and handheld tool can do it all: it can pulverize tomatoes and spices, be used to steam dishes, or even be used as a serving vessel for communal dining, a key part of West African cooking and eating.

Banku Ta

This is a wooden spatula with the ideal height and weight required to make Banku (page 173), Fufu (page 176), and other swallows. It's typically flat on both sides with round edges used to stir and create swallows with a smooth and fine texture.

Food Processor

This tool does the job of pulsing, emulsifying, and chopping much faster than a traditional mortar and pestle, knife and cutting board, or even asanka (though I keep multiple tools around for different purposes).

SEASONING BLENDS AND CONDIMENTS

The recipes that follow in this chapter are my essential cooking building blocks. My mom made her own versions using ingredients she'd buy at the market, tailoring them to our family's tastes. I do the same thing in my home and encourage you to as well. It's a smart move because making your own blend allows you to control the amount of salt and heat you're using to season your food.

Think of these seasoning blend recipes as loose parameters to guide you as you find your own version. These recipes also make enough to keep and use again and again, so feel free to scale them down to suit your own household. And in all cases you can use store-bought versions, but pay attention to the ingredients and buy the highest-quality blends with the fewest number of additives possible.

All-Day Seasoning Blend

Curry Powder (page 39)

Suya Spice Blend

ALL-DAY SEASONING BLEND

Makes a scant ¾ cup

This is the all-purpose seasoning blend I reach for in my home kitchen to flavor meats, vegetables, eggs, and just about anything else I'm looking to season with a tasty mix of spices and herbs. In the United States, "all-purpose seasoning" is the most recent name for "kitchen pepper," a customizable blend of spices that enslaved Africans used in plantation kitchens to season dishes, an ingenious shortcut that allowed cooks to add their own blend of spices to a dish quickly. You can find all-purpose seasonings like Lawry's in grocery stores, but I like making my own because I can customize the amount of spice, salt, and herbaceousness. One of my favorite ingredients to include is Worcestershire powder (a dehydrated form of the liquid kind, found readily online) because it adds a great bit of umami. If you can't find it, then it's okay to just omit it, but really try to track it down online if you can. This is a good herb-forward base, but feel free to play around with the ratios to make your own signature blend.

1 tablespoon dried parsley
1 tablespoon dried oregano
1 tablespoon kosher salt
2 teaspoons dried thyme
2 teaspoons dried rosemary
2 teaspoons whole black peppercorns
1 teaspoon cumin seeds
¼ teaspoon cayenne pepper
¼ cup sweet paprika
3 tablespoons granulated garlic
2 tablespoons granulated onion
2 teaspoons Worcestershire powder (optional)

In a mortar and pestle, spice grinder, or blender, combine the parsley, oregano, salt, thyme, rosemary, peppercorns, cumin seeds, and cayenne. Grind or blend the spices until the mixture has the same consistency as the granulated garlic. Transfer to a small bowl and whisk in the paprika, granulated garlic, granulated onion, and Worcestershire powder (if using). The seasoning will keep in an airtight container in a cool, dark place for 1 month.

SUYA SPICE BLEND

Makes about 2 cups

Suya is a peanut-based spice rub that you find all over West Africa. It's the special sauce in Chichinga (page 229), the quintessential street food in Ghana, creating a delicious combination of earthy sweetness thanks to the peanuts and a slight bitterness from the lick of flames that create a char on the meat. You can buy suya premade at any African grocer, but it's good to make your own because you can control the spice level. Suya is great on grilled meats and vegetables and even mixed into marinades to add a deep earthy flavor.

10 Maggi seasoning cubes (for sourcing, see page 31)
1½ teaspoons anise seeds
½ teaspoon whole cloves
5 grains of Selim (for sourcing, see page 26)
1 cup unsweetened peanut butter powder
¼ cup cayenne pepper
3 tablespoons ground ginger
3 tablespoons garlic powder
3 tablespoons sweet paprika
3 tablespoons onion powder

Line a baking sheet with parchment paper.

In a spice grinder or blender, combine the Maggi, anise seeds, cloves, and grains of Selim and grind until powdery. Transfer to a large pot and whisk in the peanut butter powder, cayenne, ginger, garlic powder, paprika, and onion powder.

Heat the pot over medium-low heat, stirring constantly with a wooden spoon or spatula, until the suya has darkened slightly and smells nutty and toasty, 3 to 5 minutes.

Spread the suya in an even layer on the baking sheet and cool completely. The suya will keep in an airtight container at room temperature for up to 3 months.

GINGER GARLIC PUREE

Makes 1½ cups

The smell of ginger and garlic is forever locked into my memory, instantly transporting me to my childhood. These two ingredients flavor the majority of the foods I remember eating growing up and are a big part of how I cook to this day. I don't think I'm alone in that because the blend of ginger and garlic can be found in so many international households. With this delicious combo you can build a multitude of flavors in your home. My mom would freeze batches of it and bring pieces out of the freezer for stews, marinades, and whatever else she saw fit. You can do the same to save yourself some time.

1 large hand of fresh ginger, peeled and thinly sliced crosswise
1 cup garlic cloves
½ cup plus 2 tablespoons neutral oil

In a blender, combine the ginger, garlic, and oil. Blend until completely smooth. The puree will keep in an airtight container in the refrigerator for up to 1 week or portioned in the freezer (like my mom does) for up to 3 months.

ROASTED GARLIC PUREE
Makes ½ to ¾ cup

This is a back-pocket puree that you can use in your everyday cooking to quickly add depth of flavor. I like to freeze my roasted garlic puree in ice cube trays. You can add these flavor cubes to soups, spaghetti, dips, and whatever else you want to have a sweet, earthy punch of roasted garlic. In the recipes in this book, the puree is a hack to add depth without lengthy cooking times, but honestly, I'd be hard-pressed to think of anything that does not taste better with this added. Roasted garlic puree is king in my kitchen, and I think it will be in yours too.

High-quality extra-virgin olive oil, as needed	Kosher salt and freshly ground black pepper
6 heads garlic or 1 cup garlic cloves	2 or 3 sprigs of rosemary and/or thyme

Preheat the oven to 400°F.

If using garlic heads: Drizzle a 9-inch cast-iron pan or small baking dish generously with olive oil. Cut the top ½ inch from each of the heads, exposing the cloves inside. Place in the prepared baking dish, cut sides up, then drizzle each with 1 teaspoon olive oil and sprinkle with salt and pepper. Tuck in the rosemary and/or thyme around the garlic. Cover the pan tightly with foil and roast until the garlic smells fragrant, about 35 minutes. Uncover and roast until caramelized, 10 to 20 minutes more. Transfer the garlic to a plate to cool and reserve the oil in the pan.

When cool enough to handle, squeeze the heads to push out the soft roasted garlic into the bowl of a food processor or blender. Blend until smooth, using some of the reserved garlic oil if needed to form a smooth puree.

If using garlic cloves: Place the cloves in a baking dish in an even layer and drizzle with ¼ cup olive oil. Season lightly with salt and pepper and stir to combine, then tuck in the sprigs of rosemary and/or thyme around the cloves. Cover the dish tightly with foil and bake until the garlic is sizzling and just beginning to brown on the bottom, about 20 minutes. Remove the foil, stir, and continue to roast until the garlic is golden and caramelized, 7 to 10 minutes more.

When cool enough to handle, remove the herbs, and use a slotted spoon to transfer the garlic to a food processor or blender. Blend until smooth, using some of the reserved garlic oil if needed to form a smooth puree.

The puree will keep in an airtight container in the refrigerator for up to 2 weeks or in an ice cube tray in the freezer for up to 3 months.

Note: If your blender or food processor is too large, you can puree roasted garlic using a mortar and pestle.

GREEN SEASONING
Makes 8 cups

The fresh and herbaceous hit of green seasoning is the first thing you smell when you walk into a Caribbean shop or kitchen. I love how simple and universal it is in building flavor in marinades under different names in India, Africa, and, of course, the Caribbean and Latin America. It's sort of like the uncooked version of Ghanaian Kpakoshito Sauce (Green Shito) on page 40. Green seasoning is a blend of fresh herbs and aromatics that is used to add flavor to practically anything you can think of, from salad dressings to stews. The exact ingredients vary depending on region and personal preference, but traditionally green pimento peppers and culantro, a woodier cilantro-like herb that's used in the Caribbean and Asia, are used. Green seasoning also typically includes scallions, garlic, thyme and other fresh herbs, and sometimes hot peppers—the result is especially perfect for marinades and can tenderize tough pieces of meat with the addition of vinegar or citrus.

8 small green bell peppers, stemmed, seeded, and coarsely chopped	1 cup (packed) fresh flat-leaf parsley leaves and stems
5 red or green pimento peppers or sweet baby red bell peppers, stemmed, seeded, and coarsely chopped	Leaves from 1 bunch thyme
	15 to 20 fresh culantro leaves, coarsely chopped
	15 garlic cloves
6 scallions, coarsely chopped (white and green parts)	1 to 1½ cups high-quality extra-virgin olive oil, as needed
2 shallots, coarsely chopped	

In a food processor, combine the green bell peppers, pimento peppers, scallions, shallots, parsley, thyme, culantro, garlic, and 1 cup of the oil. Blend, adding more oil if necessary, until you have a chunky consistency. The seasoning will keep in an airtight container in the refrigerator for up to 2 weeks or separated into ½-cup portions and frozen for up to 3 months.

Green Seasoning

Whether in a dry rub (*bottom*) or in a sauce (*top*), piri piri chiles are a versatile ingredient that add a pop of heat.

PIRI PIRI RUB

Makes ¼ cup

In Swahili, *piri piri* translates to "pepper-pepper," and the chili was first introduced to Mozambique via Portuguese explorers and merchants. Spicy, sweet, and smoky, the pepper now grows wild throughout the continent and can be found in recipes for sauces, marinades, and rubs like this one. Feel free to increase the piri piri if you want more heat in your rub. You can easily double or triple this recipe and it will last for weeks when stored properly.

1½ teaspoons dried oregano	1 teaspoon onion powder
2 teaspoons sweet paprika	1 teaspoon garlic powder
1 teaspoon smoked paprika	1 teaspoon ground piri piri chili (for sourcing, see page 31) or crushed dried Thai chilies
1 teaspoon ground cardamom	
1 teaspoon ground ginger	½ teaspoon kosher salt

Using a mortar and pestle or spice grinder, grind the oregano into a powder. Transfer to a small bowl and add the sweet paprika, smoked paprika, cardamom, ginger, onion powder, garlic powder, piri piri, and salt and mix until combined. The rub will keep in an airtight container in a cool, dark place for up to 1 month.

PIRI PIRI SAUCE

Makes 1½ cups

Back-to-back recipes featuring piri piri might feel like overkill, but trust me—when I think about eating in Ghana, I think about the flavor of African bird's-eye chili, also known as piri piri. Its beautiful vibrant color and crescent moon shape are an omnipresent part of the cooking there. This sauce is used in the Eggs Benedict with Scallops and Piri Piri Hollandaise (page 63) and also makes a great dressing or marinade for any proteins or vegetables.

3 to 5 piri piri chilies, depending on heat tolerance (for sourcing, see page 31), or equal quantity red Thai chilies, jalapeños, or serranos, stemmed and coarsely chopped	¼ cup red wine vinegar
	Juice of ½ lemon
	1 tablespoon fresh oregano leaves
	3 garlic cloves, plus more to taste
½ large red bell pepper, stemmed, seeded, and coarsely chopped	1½ teaspoons sweet paprika
	½ teaspoon kosher salt, plus more to taste
1 Roma tomato, cored and coarsely chopped	½ cup high-quality extra-virgin olive oil, plus more as needed
½ cup (loosely packed) coarsely chopped fresh cilantro stems	

In a blender, combine the chilies, bell pepper, tomato, cilantro, vinegar, lemon juice, oregano, garlic, paprika, and salt. Blend on low speed until smooth, then slowly add the oil with the machine running, increasing the speed to medium as you blend. Add more olive oil as needed to reach a pourable, not-too-thick sauce. Season to taste with salt. The sauce will keep in an airtight container in the refrigerator for up to 7 days or in the freezer for up to 1 month.

CURRY POWDER

Makes about 1½ cups

This is my take on curry powder, with heavy notes of fenugreek, allspice, and ginger. It mimics my favorite curry brand, Blue Mountain Country, but is dialed up on the spice so it's vibrant and has a bit of heat. If you don't want to make your own, you can buy a version that you like, such as Blue Mountain Country.

6 tablespoons coriander seeds	2 whole cloves or about ½ teaspoon ground
3 tablespoons cumin seeds	2 teaspoons fenugreek seeds, toasted and ground
3 tablespoons anise seeds	
2 tablespoons yellow mustard seeds	1¼ cups ground turmeric
	2 teaspoons ground ginger
2 tablespoons allspice berries	1 teaspoon Scotch bonnet pepper powder or cayenne pepper

Preheat the oven to 400°F.

On a rimmed baking sheet, combine the coriander seeds, cumin seeds, anise seeds, mustard seeds, allspice berries, cloves, and fenugreek seeds. On a separate baking sheet, add the turmeric, ginger, and Scotch bonnet pepper powder and spread out evenly. Toast the spices, shaking the pans halfway through, until fragrant, about 5 minutes. Immediately transfer the whole spices to a bowl and let cool. Transfer the cool whole spices to a blender or spice grinder and blend until you have a fine powder. Mix with the toasted ground spices until well combined. The curry powder will keep in an airtight container at room temperature for 1 month.

SHITO

Makes 4 cups

It isn't uncommon to see shito on the dining table alongside the salt and pepper in a Ghanaian home. Similar to a Chinese XO sauce, shito is a hot-pepper condiment with a fermented funk that comes from dried herring and crayfish powder. Everyone has their secret shito recipe, and it varies from home to home. Shito should be aromatic, funky, textured, and as spicy as you want it to be. Traditionally, it is made with the native kpakpo pepper, but if that isn't available, grab a Scotch bonnet or habanero.

½ teaspoon anise seeds

½ cup smoked dried herring powder or 2 or 3 medium whole herring

¾ cup smoked dried crayfish or shrimp powder (for sourcing, see page 25)

3 medium Spanish onions, coarsely chopped

3 or 4 green kpakpo shito peppers, green Scotch bonnet peppers, or green habanero peppers (see Note)

1 (1-inch) piece of fresh ginger, peeled and coarsely chopped

5 garlic cloves

1½ cups neutral oil

5 tablespoons tomato paste

5 Maggi seasoning cubes, crushed (for sourcing, see page 31)

1 teaspoon kosher salt

½ teaspoon sweet paprika

¼ cup virgin coconut oil

In a spice grinder, grind the anise seeds until finely ground. Transfer to a bowl and set aside. If using whole herring, remove the bones and discard. In a blender, pulse the herring powder (or whole herring) and the crayfish powder until you have a coarse crumble. Transfer to the bowl with the anise and set aside. In the blender, add the onions, kpakpo shito peppers, ginger, garlic, and ¼ cup of the neutral oil and process until smooth.

In a large pot over medium-high heat, heat the remaining 1¼ cups of neutral oil. When it shimmers, add the blended vegetables. Cook, whisking constantly, until the mixture has deepened in color to warm orange, 10 to 15 minutes (you are looking to cook out the water content of the blended vegetables).

Reduce the heat to medium and add the tomato paste. Cook, stirring occasionally to prevent any scorching on the bottom of the pan, until the mixture dries out a bit, about 20 minutes. Add the fish powder mixture, crushed Maggi cubes, salt, and paprika. Continue to cook, stirring occasionally, until the shito looks and feels pasty, about 30 minutes. Remove from the heat and stir in the coconut oil. The shito will keep in an airtight container in the refrigerator for 1 month.

Note: If you can't find any of the fresh green chilies called for, use 1 heaping tablespoon of crushed red pepper flakes instead. Add half the pepper flakes to the spice grinder with the anise seeds in the first step and proceed with the recipe, adding all the pepper flakes to the pot with the rest of the spices.

KPAKOSHITO SAUCE
Green Shito

Makes 2 cups

This condiment makes me think of late nights in Accra eating yam chips and fried fish after an evening of bouncing around Bloom Bar, Ace, and other late-night spots. Kpakoshito sauce is a variation of the traditional shito sauce but uses green kpakpo peppers and aromatics as the star ingredients, versus the dried herring and crayfish powders in shito. Green shito is very spicy and is brighter in color and in flavor with the inclusion of herbs like basil and cilantro. It's excellent as a spicy condiment or can be used as a spice enhancer for marinades. You can order kpakpo peppers online through various sites like Etsy or even find kpakoshito at specialty spice retailers like TheAfroBodega.com.

1 large yellow onion, coarsely chopped

2 green Anaheim peppers or poblanos, stemmed, seeded, and coarsely chopped

1 green bell pepper, stemmed, seeded, and coarsely chopped

8 green kpakpo shito peppers, green Scotch bonnet peppers, or green habaneros, stemmed

½ cup (packed) coarsely chopped fresh cilantro

3 fresh basil leaves with stems, coarsely chopped

5 scallions, coarsely chopped (green parts only)

5 garlic cloves

2 (thumb-size) pieces of fresh ginger, peeled and coarsely chopped

2 Maggi seasoning cubes (for sourcing, see page 31)

2 teaspoons dried rosemary

1½ cups avocado oil

Kosher salt

In a blender or food processor, combine the onion, Anaheim peppers, bell pepper, kpakpo shito peppers, cilantro, basil, scallions, garlic, ginger, Maggi cubes, rosemary, and ¼ cup of water. Blend until completely smooth.

In a large pot over medium-high heat, heat the avocado oil. When it shimmers, add the pepper mixture and cook, stirring often, until the mixture has deepened in color and the oil settles on top, 8 to 10 minutes. Season to taste with salt.

The sauce will keep in an airtight container in the refrigerator for up to 10 days or in the freezer for 2 months.

Kpakoshito Sauce (Green Shito) (*left*)
and Shito (*right*)

MOM'S HOT PEPPER SAUCE
Makes about 2 cups

This was the go-to hot sauce in my home growing up. I remember watching my mom make this so quickly, as if she knew it like the back of her hand, because she kinda did. In my memories, my mother would simply pulse her ingredients to make something similar to a chutney. Vinegar was used for the big batches to help preserve it, or water if she wanted to make a quick batch to spice up whatever she was eating that day. This is her same recipe but pureed into a hot sauce. Be warned: a little goes a long way. You can use the same pickling liquid for other kinds of pickles too, like pickled onions.

- 1 tablespoon high-quality extra-virgin olive oil
- 2 Scotch bonnet or habanero peppers, stemmed
- ½ small yellow onion, finely diced
- 1 garlic clove
- 1 (½-inch) piece of fresh ginger, peeled and coarsely chopped
- 1 Roma tomato, finely diced
- ¾ cup Pickling Liquid (recipe follows)
- 1 teaspoon kosher salt

In a small pot over medium-high heat, heat the oil. When the oil shimmers, add the peppers, onion, garlic, and ginger and cook, stirring, until the vegetables are soft, 3 to 5 minutes. Stir in the tomato and cook until the tomato has softened and released some of its liquid, about an additional 10 minutes. Add the pickling liquid, ½ cup of water, and the salt, then allow to simmer until everything is soft, about 20 minutes. Transfer to a blender, and with the lid slightly cracked to allow steam to escape, blend until smooth.

The hot sauce will keep in an airtight nonreactive container in the refrigerator for up to 1 month.

Note: To make this more of a chutney, use 6 tablespoons of pickling liquid and ¼ cup of water. Pulse in the blender to your desired consistency.

Pickling Liquid
Makes 2½ cups

This liquid adds a tart back note to the hot pepper sauce but can also be used to pickle veggies like carrots, onions, and cucumbers.

- 1 cup white wine vinegar
- 1 cup sugar
- 2½ tablespoons kosher salt
- 1 (2-inch) piece of fresh ginger, thinly sliced
- 2 fresh bay leaves
- 1 star anise pod
- 1 cinnamon stick
- 2 allspice berries

In a medium pot over medium heat, bring the vinegar and ½ cup of water to a boil. Add the sugar and salt and whisk to dissolve, then remove the pot from the heat. Add the ginger, bay leaves, star anise, cinnamon stick, and allspice berries. Cover and let steep for 30 minutes. Strain through a fine-mesh sieve and let cool. The pickling liquid will keep in an airtight container in the refrigerator for up to 2 weeks.

BREAKFAST

A West African Household
in New York

To understand where I come from and why I love food, you have to know about one person: my mom, Abena Agyeman. She was born in Kumasi, Ghana, known as the cultural capital of the country. Her first name, Abena, is the name that is given to girls born on a Tuesday. She's one of six kids and left the country to move to America for work in the 1980s, eventually landing in New York City and working at a hospital in Manhattan. She has great emotional intelligence and always knows when people are BS-ing her. She's easily one of the smartest and funniest people I know.

Growing up, I'd watch her move through the compact kitchen in my family's modestly sized, split-level home in Yonkers, where it felt like there were an endless number of nooks and crannies for all of the tools and ingredients she needed to cook. She'd open a cabinet and boom—her asanka, an earthenware bowl and handheld tool like a large mortar and pestle, would be out and ready to grind, mash, and mix ingredients. My mom has had her asanka since the 1980s, and I remember watching her use it to make our dinners, adding fresh ingredients like onion, garlic, peppers, and tomatoes and rhythmically processing the ingredients into a paste.

Sometimes she'd pull enough yams or plantains to feed our group of eight from a large woven metal basket on the floor. Or she'd open the cabinet under the sink and scoop white rice out of a plastic tub, big enough to hold the 50-pound bags we'd buy from the grocery store. Other times she'd reach up to the top shelf where she kept her favorite spices, like cardamom, ground ginger, cayenne, nutmeg, and clove, that she'd use to flavor dishes or combine to make her own spice blends.

Although my mom did occasionally make spaghetti or hamburgers to try to incorporate American culture into our home, our West African kitchen in New York mostly was a place where dishes made a faraway home reachable and tangible for all of us.

That home in Yonkers held two families. Upstairs was my family: my mom, my stepdad, my brothers, Kwadwo (Edward) and Barffuor (BB), and my sister, Maame Nyarko (Evelyn). Downstairs was my aunty Agatha, her husband, Uncle Joe, and their four children, Tony, Adela, Maybel, and Faith. Eating together was a weekly tradition growing up. On Sundays after church, my whole extended family would hang out at the house and have a big dinner. It was often chaotic, like the first scene of *Home Alone*, where you're dropped into the McCallister household with children running through the house and parents trying to get things done around them. My cousins and I would run up and down the stairs, or even slide down the stairs on couch cushions or pillows, two at a time, while my uncle yelled at us to stop because it was loud and he couldn't hear the television.

Music was a must. Sometimes it was Ghanaian gospel music, but oftentimes it was Daddy Lumba (he was like the Lionel Richie of Ghana back in the day). Lumba was a big part of my childhood—I remember going to gatherings and birthday parties or any sort of get-together in other West African homes and Lumba would be on repeat. That's what my parents and the elders got down to. That, and Pat Thomas. Pat Thomas has a song called "Sika Ye Mogya," which translates to "Money Is Blood." My family told me that in Ghana, they would play the song every afternoon when the lottery picks were announced. In the United States, my mom always played it and sang along because it reminded her of home, which, I'm sure, she missed.

Kumasi, Ghana, and the whole region of West Africa really felt like the heartbeat of our family life, a current that flowed through our house in so many ways. It was in how my mother and aunt spoke Twi to one another while they caught up on the week's goings-on over tea. It was in the music playing. It was in the artwork in my house, the wooden carvings of birds and giraffes, and the photographs of family members, of weddings, and of my mom in her younger years in Ghana. But most distinctly, it showed up in our kitchen and the dishes my mother would make for our family, and how we ate together. A big pot of jollof rice with a slow-simmered protein in a tomato sauce was a dinner staple. Everyone thinks their mom's jollof is the best in the world, but I can say, without question, that my mom's is legendary. I know this because whenever there's a community event like a birthday, anniversary, or basically any gathering of West African people from my church, people ask her to bring her jollof. If you know Africans, you know that's a high honor.

My favorite foods growing up were traditional dishes like fried yams with shito and spicy tomato pepper sauce or fried tilapia with kenkey, a fermented baseball-sized swallow. To eat it, you pull a piece of kenkey off with your left hand and scoop up a bit of sauce before putting it into your mouth. It was always perfect. It has always impressed me how my mom can take just two, three, four, maybe five basic ingredients and put them together to create a truly amazing meal. I think the best cooks do that.

Looking back, I can see that the labor of cooking dishes was about her showing us love, but it was also about giving us a connection to Ghana and our culture, even from Yonkers. The laborious nature of some of the most iconic dishes of West Africa taught me about the ways in which food should not be rushed. Watching my mom start dishes in the afternoon for dinner taught me that the stews, soups, and sauces needed the chance to reveal themselves and meld. It takes lengthy cooking times to extract deep, rich flavors from bones, to make proteins or vegetables tender enough to be eaten with the hand, to make sure that the spice level is just right. There's a long tradition of taking your time with food in West African cooking, instead of forcing it to be done as quickly as possible, that runs through dishes like tangy braised chicken yassa, or complex and earthy palm nut soup. Beloved dishes throughout the African diaspora, like Brazil's earthy feijoada, made of black beans and pork pieces simmered until they're falling apart, or spiced oxtail stew in the Caribbean, or stews of pig feet or pork neck bones in the American South, also showcase that technique.

The idea of being "other" in America is complicated for me as a West African. I can empathize with different immigrant or "third culture" stories, but they don't feel like they quite match my experience because I see so much West African influence in American foods and culture. Being born here and immersed in it since childhood allowed me to move through life differently than my mother, who came here as an adult. Looking back, I think about how hard it must have been for her to emotionally navigate a new country as a mom and an immigrant. As a kid, I saw firsthand how people she interacted with would treat her differently once they heard her accent. It felt like there was an assumption that she wasn't smart or intellectual. It made me feel protective over her, and I wanted to shield her from these microaggressions. I know now how common my mom's experience is, for people of many backgrounds. It feels like there's this American mentality toward immigrants that says you're not good enough, or that you're not smart, or that you're not like us because you weren't born here. I've always known that isn't right and doesn't make sense.

But in our home, my mom made sure our cultural compass was oriented toward Ghana and the flavors, sounds, and sights of West Africa. We were clear on that being a part of who we were because it enveloped us and all of our senses at home. Knowing that part of my heritage helped create a home base for me and a sense of safety to explore other cultures and parts of the world.

To this day, my mom is continuing to provide that base for our family. Now with her eight grandchildren, she's always asking them if they're hungry and if they've eaten, at intervals of what feels like thirty minutes. They'll be running around as children do, and she's thinking about their bellies and what she can cook for them. It's still how she shows love.

Spiced Fonio Porridge
with Coconut (page 52)

Ablemamu (Tom
Brown Porridge)

ABLEMAMU
Tom Brown Porridge

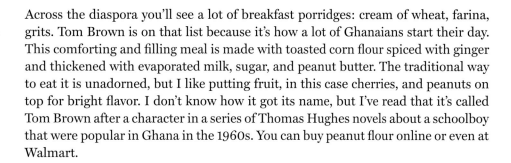

Serves 4

Across the diaspora you'll see a lot of breakfast porridges: cream of wheat, farina, grits. Tom Brown is on that list because it's how a lot of Ghanaians start their day. This comforting and filling meal is made with toasted corn flour spiced with ginger and thickened with evaporated milk, sugar, and peanut butter. The traditional way to eat it is unadorned, but I like putting fruit, in this case cherries, and peanuts on top for bright flavor. I don't know how it got its name, but I've read that it's called Tom Brown after a character in a series of Thomas Hughes novels about a schoolboy that were popular in Ghana in the 1960s. You can buy peanut flour online or even at Walmart.

1¼ cups corn flour

½ cup peanut flour

½ cup chopped palm sugar from a block or light brown sugar, plus more to taste

1 cup evaporated milk, plus more for serving

1 tablespoon unsalted natural creamy peanut butter

½ teaspoon ground cinnamon

¼ teaspoon ground ginger

¼ teaspoon ground nutmeg

1 cup sweet cherries, stemmed, pitted, and finely chopped, or frozen cherries, for serving (optional)

3 tablespoons roasted peanuts, skins removed, chopped, for serving (optional)

Preheat the oven to 375°F.

Combine the corn flour and peanut flour on a rimmed baking sheet. Toast, stirring every few minutes, until lightly browned and fragrant, 10 to 12 minutes.

Transfer the flours to a medium pot. Add 2 cups of water and whisk until well combined. Set the pot over medium heat and cook, whisking constantly, until slightly thickened and no longer raw-tasting, 7 to 10 minutes. Add the sugar, evaporated milk, peanut butter, cinnamon, ginger, and nutmeg. Whisk well to combine, then continue to cook until you have a smooth, semi-thick paste, 2 to 3 minutes longer. Taste and add more sugar if you like.

Divide the porridge among 4 bowls. Top with chopped cherries and peanuts (if using), and drizzle with more evaporated milk. Serve hot or warm.

SPICED FONIO PORRIDGE
with Coconut

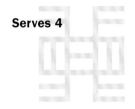

Serves 4

Fonio, a small grain with a texture similar to couscous when cooked, is indigenous to West Africa and is considered to be the oldest cereal on the continent. The grain's uses are endless, and for so many, eating fonio porridge brings back beloved childhood memories. I always credit fonio's availability in America to chefs like Pierre Thiam and Jessica B. Harris, who incorporate fonio into their menus and cookbooks, helping to spread the gospel of the grain's nutritional benefits and low environmental impact. I love this porridge because the fonio gets time to develop an amazing nutty and sweet flavor that is hearty, yet it's easy to make at home.

1 cup fonio (for sourcing, see page 26)

2 cinnamon sticks

3 green cardamom pods

2 whole cloves

1 (13.5-ounce) can full-fat coconut milk

2 tablespoons agave syrup, plus more for serving

Kosher salt

Sliced fresh strawberries, mango, banana, blueberries, and/or dried coconut flakes, for serving

In a fine-mesh sieve, rinse the fonio using lukewarm water until the water runs clear.

In a medium pot over medium heat, combine the cinnamon sticks, cardamom pods, and cloves. Toast, stirring often, until fragrant, 2 minutes. Add 4 cups of water and bring to a boil. Stir in the fonio. Raise the heat to medium-high and bring to a simmer. Cook, stirring constantly, until the fonio has absorbed the water and becomes a thick porridge, about 5 minutes. Reduce the heat to medium-low. Add the coconut milk and agave. Taste and add a pinch of salt, if you'd like. If you like the consistency, serve immediately. Otherwise, continue to cook, stirring, until thickened but still slightly loose, 5 to 7 minutes more.

Remove and discard the cinnamon sticks, cardamom pods, and cloves. Divide the porridge among 4 bowls, top with the fruit of your choice, and drizzle with more agave. Serve immediately.

CASSAVA PANCAKES
with Malted Barley Crumble

Serves 4

My love for pancakes runs deep. I adored them as a kid when my mom would make a batch, and I cooked them religiously while in high school from a box mix. Eventually I was brave enough to try my hand at my own homemade mix, and I've never looked back. Cassava, also known as yuca, is an extremely versatile tuber that's used throughout Africa and the Americas for countless dishes, from stews and mashes to yuca fries. Cassava flour is used as the base of my batter with a small amount of cornmeal to help create pancakes that are fluffy with a bit of crunch and crispy edges. A crumble made from Grape-Nuts cereal, another familiar ingredient, adds a buttery sweet crunch to your pancakes. Serve this with some butter and maple syrup to finish—delightful.

Crumble

¾ cup Grape-Nuts cereal

4 tablespoons (½ stick) unsalted butter, melted

1 tablespoon (packed) light brown sugar

1 tablespoon maple syrup

1 teaspoon kosher salt

½ teaspoon ground cinnamon

Pancakes

1⅓ cups cassava flour

3 tablespoons finely ground cornmeal

2½ tablespoons granulated sugar

1 tablespoon baking powder

2 teaspoons kosher salt

1½ cups whole milk

2 large eggs

½ teaspoon vanilla bean paste or vanilla extract

4 tablespoons (½ stick) unsalted butter, melted and cooled, plus more for brushing the griddle

Salted butter, for serving

Maple syrup, for serving

Preheat the oven to 200°F.

Make the crumble: In a medium bowl, mix the Grape-Nuts, melted butter, brown sugar, maple syrup, salt, and cinnamon until well combined. Set aside.

Make the pancakes: In another medium bowl, whisk together the cassava flour, cornmeal, granulated sugar, baking powder, and salt and set aside. In a large bowl, whisk together the milk, eggs, and vanilla bean paste. Gradually add the dry mixture to the wet and keep whisking until your batter just comes together. Do not overmix—a few small lumps are okay. Pour in the cooled melted butter and whisk gently to incorporate. Set the batter aside to rest for 5 minutes to give the cassava flour time to hydrate.

Heat a griddle or medium skillet over medium heat until a bit of water dropped into the pan evaporates quickly, about 2 minutes. Brush about 1 teaspoon of melted butter on the griddle, then spoon ¼-cup portions of batter onto the griddle and leave untouched until you see air bubbles form on the surface of the pancakes, about 2 minutes. Flip and cook on the other side until golden, about 2 minutes more. Move the cooked pancakes to a rimmed baking sheet and transfer to the oven to keep warm while you finish off the batter. Wipe the griddle clean of any browned butter with a paper towel, then repeat with more melted butter and the remaining batter as needed, toggling between medium and medium-low heat to ensure the pancakes are golden but not too dark.

To serve, top the pancakes with the crumble, salted butter, and maple syrup. Serve immediately.

SUGAR BREAD

Makes 1 loaf

My sister, Maame Nyarko, always has sugar bread in her home, and anytime I visit, I make a beeline straight to the bread, grab some butter from her fridge, and find a pan to toast it up just the way I like. Sugar bread is commonly eaten during breakfast and as a snack in Ghana. Similar to a Portuguese sweet bread, it's yeasty and sweet, of course, and depending on where in the country, flavored with notes of cinnamon, nutmeg, or even pineapple extract. It's difficult to pinpoint how exactly this bread got to the country, but I'm sure glad it's here.

1 cup (240g) lukewarm water (100°–110°F)

5 teaspoons active dry yeast

1 cup (110g) confectioners' sugar

3 cups (410g) bread flour, plus more for dusting

3 tablespoons unsalted butter, melted, plus more for the pan and 1 tablespoon for brushing

1 teaspoon kosher salt

1 teaspoon vanilla extract

½ teaspoon ground nutmeg

½ teaspoon neutral oil

In a small bowl or measuring cup, combine the warm water, yeast, and 1 teaspoon of the sugar. Whisk gently to combine and set aside until frothy and foamy, about 5 minutes.

In a stand mixer fitted with the dough hook attachment, add the remaining sugar, the flour, melted butter, salt, vanilla, and nutmeg. Mix on medium-low speed until the mixture is crumbly, about 3 minutes. Add the lukewarm yeast mixture and continue to mix on medium-low speed until a tight dough ball forms that pulls away from the sides of the bowl, about 10 minutes. Lightly flour a work surface and turn out the dough. Knead until the dough is elastic and silky, about 10 minutes.

Place the dough in a large bowl greased with the oil, cover with plastic wrap, and allow to proof in a warm place until doubled in size, 40 minutes to 1 hour. Meanwhile, butter and flour a 9 × 5 bread loaf pan.

Lightly flour a work surface, your hands, and a rolling pin. Take the dough out of the bowl and punch it down to release the air. Roll the dough out into a large rectangle, about 8 × 15 inches. Starting at one of the short edges, roll the dough until you have an 8-inch log and place it in the prepared pan. Cover loosely with plastic wrap and proof until doubled in size, about 40 minutes.

While the dough proofs, position a rack in the middle of the oven and preheat the oven to 350°F. Remove the plastic and bake the loaf until golden and a thermometer inserted into the center reads 190°F, about 35 minutes. Melt the remaining 1 tablespoon of butter.

As soon as the bread comes out of the oven, brush the melted butter over the top. After 5 minutes, carefully turn out the loaf onto a cooling rack. Cover with a clean kitchen towel and allow to cool for at least 1 hour before slicing. Once completely cool, the bread will keep for 3 days wrapped tightly in plastic wrap.

EGUSI AND COCONUT GRANOLA

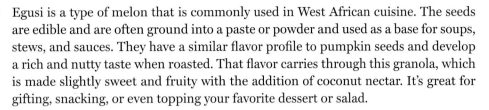

Makes about 3½ cups Egusi is a type of melon that is commonly used in West African cuisine. The seeds are edible and are often ground into a paste or powder and used as a base for soups, stews, and sauces. They have a similar flavor profile to pumpkin seeds and develop a rich and nutty taste when roasted. That flavor carries through this granola, which is made slightly sweet and fruity with the addition of coconut nectar. It's great for gifting, snacking, or even topping your favorite dessert or salad.

1¼ cups old-fashioned oats

½ cup blanched sliced almonds

3 tablespoons egusi seeds (for sourcing, see page 26)

3 tablespoons flaxseeds

1 tablespoon fresh thyme leaves

1½ teaspoons ground cinnamon

1 teaspoon kosher salt

¼ cup virgin coconut oil

2 tablespoons glucose syrup or light corn syrup

2 tablespoons coconut nectar or maple syrup

¼ teaspoon vanilla bean paste or vanilla extract

Preheat the oven to 300°F. Line a rimmed baking sheet with parchment paper or a Silpat baking mat.

In a large bowl, combine the oats, almonds, egusi seeds, flaxseeds, thyme, cinnamon, and salt. Set aside.

In a medium pot over low heat, combine the coconut oil, glucose syrup, coconut nectar, and vanilla bean paste. Cook, whisking constantly, until well combined and warmed through, about 3 minutes. Pour the warm oil mixture over the dry ingredients and mix to coat well.

Spread the mixture in an even layer on the prepared baking sheet. Bake, stirring every 30 minutes to ensure even toasting, until the granola is mostly dry (it will continue to crisp out of the oven) and smells toasty, about 2 hours.

Let the granola cool completely before storing in an airtight container for up to 1 month.

BISCUITS
with Guava Thyme Jam

Serves 4 to 6

I find a lot of joy in creatively pairing culturally significant ingredients and dishes to make a cohesive meal, and this biscuit and guava thyme jam combination does exactly that. Guava is a delicious fruit that grows on small trees that can be found across tropical climates, but especially in the Caribbean. Paired with thyme, an essential herb that you'll find throughout Caribbean cooking, this jam is a sweet, fruity ode to the flavors of the Caribbean and is a great addition to your breakfast rotation—on toast, as a base for a glaze or vinaigrette, or served with cheese. The biscuit is laminated with butter, creating a crispy exterior and a flaky interior that, when cut open, is the perfect vessel for the sweet and fragrant jam. I like using White Lily flour because it has a good amount of gluten which makes for a strong biscuit with a crunchy exterior and soft interior. If you can't find it, any self-rising flour will do the trick.

Jam

2 cups sugar

¼ cup powdered pectin

3 pounds ripe pink guavas or 2 pounds frozen pink guava pulp, thawed

3 fresh bay leaves

4 sprigs of thyme

1 tablespoon fresh lime juice

½ teaspoon kosher salt

Biscuits

3½ cups (420g) all-purpose flour, plus more for dusting

2 tablespoons sugar

1 tablespoon baking powder

2 teaspoons kosher salt

½ teaspoon baking soda

1¼ cups (2½ sticks / 285g) cold unsalted butter, cut into small cubes

1¼ cups (300g) cold buttermilk

1 large egg

Special Equipment

3 (10-ounce) canning jars with lids, or 2 (16-ounce) jars

Make the jam: In a small bowl, combine the sugar and pectin and mix well. Set aside.

If using fresh fruit, using a vegetable peeler, peel the guavas. Trim them by removing the stem and bottom; remove any blemishes. Cut the guavas in half crosswise then use a spoon to remove any seeds from the center. Cut the guavas into ½-inch chunks and transfer to a food processor. Pulse until slightly chunky (it should resemble tomato puree); you should have 2 pounds of guava fruit. If using frozen guava pulp, start at the next step.

In a large pot, combine the guava with the bay leaves and thyme. Pour the sugar mixture over the fruit and bring to a boil over medium-high heat. Stirring occasionally, cook until the mixture is thick and no longer runny, 20 to 25 minutes. Cool for 10 minutes. Remove the bay leaves and thyme from the pot then season with the lime juice and salt.

While the jam cooks, sterilize the jars (see Notes, page 62). Place the jars and lids in a large pot and cover with water until submerged. Bring to a simmer over medium-high heat and let simmer for 10 minutes. Keep the jars in the water until ready to fill. One at a time, carefully remove the jars with tongs, pouring out the water from the interior, and place them on a clean, heat-resistant surface. Cover and reserve the pot of simmering water.

Recipe continues

Divide the jam among the jars, filling each up to ½ inch from the lid (if there's any excess, serve immediately or discard). Stir each jar of jam with a clean nonreactive spatula or chopstick to pop any air bubbles. Seal the lids, return the jars to the pot of water, and cover. Boil the jars in the water for 20 minutes. Remove the jars from the boiling water, set upright on a kitchen towel, and let cool for 30 minutes. The jam will keep in an airtight container in the refrigerator for up to 3 months.

Position a rack in the lower third of the oven and preheat the oven to 425°F. Line a baking sheet with parchment paper.

Make the biscuits: Sift the flour, sugar, baking powder, salt, and baking soda into a large bowl. Using a pastry blender, cut the butter into the flour mixture until it becomes crumbly and the pieces of butter are the size of peas. With gloves on or with a wooden spoon, mix in the cold buttermilk until a shaggy dough forms. Lightly flour a work surface and dump out the dough. Knead the dough 3 or 4 times, just until it comes together. Pat the dough into a ½-inch thick rectangle then cut in half. Stack one half on top of the other and pat the dough back into a ½-inch thick rectangle.

Fill a shallow dish with flour and dip a 3-inch biscuit cutter in the flour. Then, cut out as many biscuits as you can from the dough by pushing straight down and lifting up (see Notes). Gently rework any scraps to cut out 1 or 2 more biscuits; you should have 10 to 12 total. Place the biscuits on the prepared baking sheet, allowing them to touch each other. In a small bowl, lightly beat the egg to create an egg wash, then brush the top of each biscuit with the egg.

Bake until the biscuits have risen, spread a little, and are lightly golden in color, 12 to 15 minutes. Remove the baking sheet from the oven and let cool slightly on a wire rack, then serve the biscuits warm with jam.

Notes: You can sterilize the jars either in boiling water as directed above or in a 250°F oven for 20 minutes. Then fill, boil, cool, and refrigerate as directed.

Biscuits can be frozen once they've been punched out of the dough. Freeze on a baking sheet until solid, then place in a resealable plastic bag and freeze for up to 6 months. Remove from the freezer to defrost slightly before baking as directed.

EGGS BENEDICT
with Scallops and Piri Piri Hollandaise

Serves 4

You know what excites me? Brunch! I'm a big fan, and one of my favorite things to order is eggs Benedict, so I wanted to create a recipe that pairs something people may not be familiar with (the piri piri chili, a big part of West African cooking) with something people may recognize (buttery hollandaise). Serving it with seared scallops just puts it over the top. Piri piri adds a floral yet sharp heat that cuts the richness of the sauce. This is a great dish for a weekend morning when you have a bit more time.

Hollandaise

2 cups hot water, plus more as needed

1¼ cups (2½ sticks) unsalted butter, plus more as needed

4 large egg yolks

2 tablespoons fresh lemon juice, plus more to taste

Kosher salt

¼ to ½ cup Piri Piri Sauce (page 39), depending on your heat tolerance

Poached Eggs

3 tablespoons distilled white vinegar

4 large eggs

Scallops

4 large (U10) scallops

Kosher salt

Neutral oil

2 English muffins, split and toasted, for serving

Small handful of baby spinach leaves, for serving

Make the hollandaise: Fill a blender with the hot water and set aside to warm.

Meanwhile, in a small saucepan over medium heat, melt the butter until foaming. Cover to keep warm and set aside.

In a medium saucepan over medium-high heat, bring a few inches of water to a simmer. Fit a medium metal or glass bowl in the pot and make sure it isn't touching the water. Put the egg yolks in the bowl. Holding the edge of the bowl with a dry kitchen towel or pot holder, whisk the egg yolks constantly until they are slightly opaque, about 2 minutes. (We want to gently cook the eggs so that they thicken slightly without scrambling.) Remove the bowl from the pot; reserve the pot of water.

Discard the hot water from the blender, then pour in the egg yolks and lemon juice. Blend until combined. Working quickly and with the blender running on medium-high speed, slowly pour the warm butter into the blender in a very thin stream. Blend until a creamy sauce forms. (If the hollandaise doesn't have the right consistency, adjusting it is easy: with the blender running, slowly add hot water to loosen or melted butter 1 tablespoon at a time to thicken.) Taste and season with more lemon juice, if needed, and salt. Transfer the sauce to a medium bowl and whisk in the piri piri sauce. Cover to keep warm while you poach the eggs.

Poach the eggs: To the same pot of water you used to cook the egg yolks, add the vinegar and more water, if needed, to fill the pot halfway. Bring to a gentle boil over medium-high heat. Line a plate with paper towels.

Recipe continues

Crack 1 egg into a small bowl and set aside. Fill a medium bowl with warm water. Create a whirlpool in the pot of boiling water by stirring the water clockwise with a slotted spoon. Gently pour the egg into the center of the whirlpool while continuing to gently stir clockwise around the edge of the pot until the egg white surrounds the yolk. Cook for 3 minutes for a runny egg or 4 minutes for a medium egg. Using the slotted spoon, transfer the egg to the paper towel–lined plate. Repeat with the remaining eggs. Carefully transfer the poached eggs to the bowl of warm water to maintain their temperature.

Make the scallops: Make sure that the scallops are clean and free of their attachment muscle. (To remove, simply peel away the strip of muscle on the side of each scallop and discard.) Pat the scallops very dry with paper towels and season with salt. Line a plate with paper towels.

Coat a medium sauté pan or skillet with enough oil to cover the entire pan in a thin layer, then heat the oil over medium-high heat until it shimmers. Add the scallops in a single layer and sear, undisturbed, until golden brown on the bottom, about 4 minutes. Flip the scallops and cook until the second side is warmed through, about 1 minute. Transfer the scallops to the prepared plate.

To serve, arrange the English muffin halves on plates. Divide the spinach among the muffins, then top each with a scallop and an egg. Spoon the hollandaise over the top. Serve immediately.

ROASTED BANANA GRITS
with Seasoned Shrimp

Serves 6

I won't touch the "sweet-versus-salty-grits" debate, so I made these banana grits that combine a bit of both. I know, I know—hear me out. I actually dislike the taste of raw bananas, but when a banana gets roasted or baked, it acquires a wonderful buttery, caramelized depth of flavor. This recipe was born in Ghana for East End Bistro, a casual restaurant in Accra for which I consulted on the opening menu. In Ghana, bananas are shorter and quite stubby, and pack so much sweetness. We received what seemed like a ton of these bananas from our purveyor, and my first idea was to roast most of them and use the puree as a base for our brunch service, where some of the best sweet-savory dishes live. The roasted banana brings a unique flavor to the grits that's well balanced by garlic and shallots. The grits are finished with a soft cheese that complements their texture and creates a creamy lusciousness at the same time.

This is a perfect brunch party dish when served with shrimp and a poached or fried egg on each plate. Leftover grits can be used to make griddled grit cakes or saved and warmed for later.

Grits

- 3 medium ripe bananas in their peels
- 2 tablespoons neutral oil
- 4 tablespoons (½ stick) unsalted butter
- 5 garlic cloves, minced
- 1 large shallot, finely diced
- 4 cups whole milk
- 1 cup heavy cream
- 1 cup reduced-sodium chicken stock, plus more as needed
- ¼ cup sugar
- 1 teaspoon kosher salt
- 2 cups white stone-ground grits (medium or finely ground)
- 2 tablespoons mascarpone

Shrimp

- 1 tablespoon neutral oil
- 12 large (U16–20; about ¾ pound) shrimp, peeled with the tail left on, and deveined
- 2 tablespoons All-Day Seasoning Blend (page 35)
- Kosher salt
- 6 scallions, thinly sliced (white and green parts), for garnish
- Fried eggs, for serving (optional)

Preheat the oven to 400°F.

Make the grits: Place the bananas on a rimmed baking sheet and roast, flipping the bananas halfway through, until the skins are evenly dark, 10 to 20 minutes. Allow to cool on the baking sheet. When they're cool enough to handle, peel and place in a blender. Blend, adding water by the teaspoon as needed, to create a puree. You should have about 1½ cups. Set aside.

In a large pot, heat the oil and 2 tablespoons of the butter over medium-low heat until the butter starts to melt. Add the garlic and shallot and sauté, stirring, until the vegetables soften and become fragrant, 3 to 5 minutes. Raise the heat to medium-high, then add the milk, cream, chicken stock, sugar, and salt and bring to a boil.

Recipe continues

Gradually add the grits while whisking. Once the grits are fully incorporated, reduce the heat to low. Cook the grits, whisking frequently and adding a bit more stock or water a few tablespoons at a time if the grits become too dry, until completely tender, about 20 minutes. Pull the pot off the heat. Whisk in ½ cup of the banana puree, the remaining 2 tablespoons of butter, and the mascarpone. Add more banana puree for more pronounced flavor. Set aside and keep warm. (Leftover banana puree will keep in an airtight container in the refrigerator for up to 5 days.)

Make the shrimp: In a large sauté pan, heat the oil over medium-high heat until shimmering. In a large bowl, toss the shrimp with the seasoning blend and a pinch of salt. Add the shrimp to the pan and cook, stirring often, until they are pink and cooked through, 2 to 4 minutes. Remove from the heat.

Divide the roasted banana grits among 6 bowls. Add 2 shrimp to each bowl, garnish with scallions and a fried egg if desired, and serve right away.

SNACKS AND DRINKS

Seeing New York—and the World—with My Dad

One day when I was about seven or eight years old and was playing with my younger brother, BB, at home in Yonkers, we knocked over a box in my mom's room. Out fell a photograph of my mom, me as a baby, and a tall dark-skinned man I didn't recognize but whose features resembled my own. I showed my mom the photo and asked who the man was. She confirmed what I instinctively understood: my stepfather wasn't my dad, and this man in the photo was my biological father. As a kid, I accepted and respected my stepfather, who took on the role of dad, but with that said, he wasn't my biological father.

Less than a week later, the man from the photograph appeared in our living room. I didn't ask my mom to invite him; I just think she wanted to do it. I was so nervous. I don't recall if we hugged or shook hands, but I know we embraced and I remember feeling shy. I just kept looking at his face: he looked just like that photo, just like me. From there, we developed a relationship and started spending time together. Finding that photo of my father, Benjamin Akwasi Adjepong, changed my life.

My father lived in the Bronx and worked as a taxi driver in New York City. On weekends, he would pick me up and drive me around the city in his cab, playing tour guide and showing me landmarks. We would drive by Madison Square Garden and see Knicks fans going to games, or the old Yankee Stadium, the Bronx Zoo, the Empire State Building, and Times Square. Once or twice, he picked up a passenger while we were hanging out, but mostly it would be the two of us, me in the front seat looking through the windows at the city as it went by. He knew the city so well, and it was so cool to hear about his work and the passengers he'd had over the week. It was our time to get to know one another as father and son. He would ask me what was going on in my world and about my week, what I'd had for dinner, who my friends were, what I'd learned in school, and how my family was doing. I wasn't the most comfortable with him at first, but that time together helped us bond, and I started looking forward to it.

Our visits always included getting lunch or dinner at a place where he liked to eat when he was working. Sometimes we'd get fast food like Burger King (he loved their onion rings) or afternoon doughnuts or sweets, but mostly it was hole-in-the-wall, hot-bar buffet, mom-and-pop places. We'd take our to-go containers and eat in his taxi while catching up over Puerto Rican, West African, or Trinidadian foods. He really showed me a lot about the different cultures of New York City and the diversity of foods available in Staten Island, Queens, and Brooklyn through those meals, and the outings sparked my curiosity about the rest of the world. If the city I lived in could hold so many different flavors and experiences, then it stood to reason that the world had more for me to explore and taste. I can see how those weekends shaped me and created a love of travel. It broke up the awkwardness between a father and son who didn't know one another and gave us something to do and enjoy together.

Other than food, we loved watching basketball together. I remember watching legends like Michael Jordan, Patrick Ewing, Karl Malone, and Avery Johnson (my dad's favorite) play on TV, and I inherited my love of basketball from him.

Our relationship continued into my teenage years, when I moved from Yonkers to Wallkill upstate to stay with my aunt who had moved there. I had started to get in trouble in school, and my mom thought the move would be good for me. The distance made things tougher, but I would see him when I went to New York City to visit my mom and family.

My dad was flawed for sure, but the lessons I learned from him are becoming clearer to me now as an adult and father myself. Sometimes he wouldn't show up to our hangouts when he said he would, and it would make me feel disappointed, wondering why he didn't feel like he needed to see me. That taught me to follow through with the people who mean the most to me in my life. And he didn't really talk to me about Ghana. In hindsight, I realize he probably didn't want me to ask too many questions about him and my mother. Maybe he wanted to shield me from that story, or maybe that information would have been too much for a small child to hear. In any case, he kept that part of his life to himself.

When he died in 2005, he and I actually weren't on speaking terms. We were supposed to see one another several months before, and he didn't show up. I was mad at him and taking space for myself. Then, in 2011, my grandmother, the same one I lived with on my first trip to Ghana, passed away. Returning to Ghana to see family felt more pressing after those two losses. Although I was a broke college student, I knew I had to visit to pay my respects to not only my grandmother but also my father. I planned to visit his grave for the first time since he died six years earlier. It was my first time in Ghana as an adult.

Taking that trip with my mother, stepfather, brother, and cousins was intense. I remember feeling happy—not because of the reason for the trip but because we were all together again. When I think about it, the grief of losing my grandmother and father felt a little easier to bear because we were in Ghana, closer to extended family and people who knew them.

That trip changed my life, offering me a tremendous amount of perspective and a foundation both in my life, personally, and as a chef. The feeling of home has a strong pull wherever you go in the world, and those moments remind you of where home will always be.

Kelewele

Puna Yam Chips
(page 76)

KELEWELE

Serves 6

This is a traditional take on kelewele, which, in my mind, is a great street food. It combines the crunch of peanuts, the sweet, unctuous texture of fried plantains, and the spicy complexity of a ginger seasoning paste. It's easy to eat when you're out but is also good at home, where you can prepare it as a snack or as a side dish for a meal. For this recipe you want to avoid plantains that are black; they are the sweetest in flavor but soak up the most oil when fried!

5 grains of Selim (optional; for sourcing, see page 26)

1 teaspoon anise seeds

1 cardamom pod

1 tablespoon sweet paprika

2 teaspoons cayenne pepper

1 teaspoon ground nutmeg

1 teaspoon ground allspice

½ teaspoon kosher salt, plus more as needed

¼ teaspoon freshly ground black pepper

4 ripe yellow plantains

1 small onion, coarsely chopped

1 (1-inch) piece of fresh ginger, peeled and coarsely grated

2 garlic cloves

2 cups peanut oil, for frying

½ cup salted roasted peanuts, for garnish

In a small skillet over low heat, toast the grains of Selim (if using), anise seeds, and cardamom pod until fragrant, swirling the pan often to toast evenly, 5 to 8 minutes. Transfer the toasted spices to a spice grinder and grind to a powder. Place in a small bowl and whisk in the paprika, cayenne, nutmeg, allspice, salt, and black pepper. Set aside.

Peel the plantains by trimming about ½ inch off each end. Cut a lengthwise slit through the peel and remove and discard it. Chop the fruit into ½-inch cubes and place in a mixing bowl. To a blender, add the onion, ginger, garlic, and 2 tablespoons of water and blend until smooth. Add the blended onion mixture and spice mix to the bowl and toss well to coat evenly. Cover with plastic wrap and allow the plantains to marinate for 30 minutes at room temperature or up to 24 hours in the refrigerator.

When ready to cook, add the oil to a medium pot or cast-iron skillet. Heat over medium-high heat to 350°F. Line a plate with paper towels.

Fry the plantains in 4 batches, stirring each batch once and adjusting the heat to ensure the oil stays at temperature, until the plantains are golden and crispy, about 5 minutes. Using a spider or slotted spoon, remove the plantains to the prepared plate to drain. Sprinkle with salt. Repeat with the remaining plantains.

Transfer to a serving platter and sprinkle with roasted peanuts. Serve immediately.

PUNA YAM CHIPS

Serves 4 to 6

This bar food and popular snack in Ghana makes me think of late nights in Accra, which typically last until well after sunrise. It's pretty simple: just yam that's been fried and eaten like french fries. Depending on who you speak with or what restaurant you walk into, the terms "chips" and "fries" are used interchangeably, but both refer to the same delicious side that's crispy on the outside and tender on the inside. But I promise you, you can't have just one. Puna yam is similar to potato but has more texture and is sweeter, which makes it a great pairing for spicy Shito (page 40) and some fried fish and kebabs, which it's typically served with. If you can't find puna yam, use cassava and the same soaking process to ensure crispy fries.

2 cups hot water, plus more as needed

1½ teaspoons kosher salt, plus more for serving

1 teaspoon sugar

1 pound puna yam (about ⅓ medium yam), peeled

Neutral oil, for frying

Line a rimmed baking sheet with paper towels. In a large bowl, combine the hot water, salt, and sugar and stir to dissolve. Slice the yam in half lengthwise, then slice again crosswise. Cut each quarter into ½-inch-thick steak fries. Add the yam chips to the water; they should be completely submerged, so add a bit more water if needed to cover. Soak the yam for 30 minutes, then drain and transfer to the prepared baking sheet. Pat the yam very dry.

Fill a medium pot with 2 to 3 inches of oil and heat to 375°F over medium heat. Line another rimmed baking sheet with paper towels.

Working in batches to prevent overcrowding, fry the yam chips until they are a pale golden color, stirring often until the bubbling slows, 2 to 3 minutes. Using a spider or slotted spoon, transfer the chips to the prepared baking sheet to drain and immediately season generously with salt. Repeat with the remaining chips, letting the oil return to temperature between batches. Serve hot.

CHIN CHIN
Achomo

Serves 10

Chin chin is the snack of champions—the ultimate party nibbler. These crunchy, buttery, irresistible little fried dough bites remind me of funnel cake but are poppable. When I was growing up, chin chin showed up at every gathering in our community, often with a side of roasted peanuts. For this recipe, you can either bake or fry the chin chin, but I think frying is the better option because it results in a crispier bite with more of a warm richness than the baked option.

5½ cups all-purpose flour, plus more for dusting

1 cup plus 2 tablespoons sugar

2 teaspoons ground cinnamon

1 teaspoon ground nutmeg

½ teaspoon fine sea salt

½ teaspoon baking powder

2 large eggs

⅓ cup full-fat evaporated milk

4 tablespoons (½ stick) unsalted butter, at room temperature

3 cups avocado oil, for frying

In a large bowl, sift together the flour, sugar, cinnamon, nutmeg, salt, and baking powder. Add the eggs, evaporated milk, and butter and, using a fork, stir until the dough begins to come together.

Lightly flour a work surface and dump the dough out. Knead until the dough is elastic and slightly tacky and the butter is completely incorporated with no visible streaks remaining, about 5 minutes. Place the dough back in the bowl and cover with plastic wrap. Allow to rest for 30 minutes.

Lightly flour the work surface again and divide the dough in half. Cover one of the halves with a clean kitchen towel while working with the other. Use a rolling pin to roll out half the dough to a rough 10-inch square about ¼ inch thick. Using a pizza cutter or bench scraper, cut into ¼-inch-thick strips. Cut across the strips to make ¼-inch squares. Repeat with the other dough half.

To fry the chin chin: In a large pot over medium heat, heat the oil to 325°F. Line a rimmed baking sheet with paper towels.

Working in batches to prevent overcrowding, fry the chin chin, stirring occasionally, until evenly golden brown and puffed, 3 to 5 minutes. Using a spider or slotted spoon, transfer to the prepared baking sheet to drain. Repeat with the remaining dough, letting the oil return to temperature between each batch.

To bake the chin chin: Preheat the oven to 325°F and line 2 baking sheets with parchment paper. Divide the chin chin between the pans and bake until golden and puffed, about 20 minutes, rotating the pans halfway through.

Serve hot. Fully cooled chin chin will keep in an airtight container at room temperature for 5 days.

DAD'S ONION RINGS
with Zip Sauce

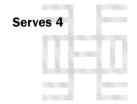

Serves 4

This recipe is a thank-you to my dad, Benjamin Adjepong. Whenever I have onion rings, I think back to those Sundays in his taxicab exploring New York City together, and memories of all the things we saw and tasted in the boroughs flash through my mind. I'm so thankful for those Sunday car rides: the heart-to-heart conversations, basketball talk, and just enjoying each other's company. In retrospect, those few hours each Sunday helped shape my point of view on food today because they showed me different cultures and how delicious food can come from anywhere. Although our trips were often occupied with meals from the many cuisines available in the city, the real source of comfort to my dad was the onion rings from Burger King. Since my dad isn't here in the flesh to see how he impacted me or this cookbook, I honored him as best as I could with this recipe. The zip sauce is my own creation, adding a creamy, tangy component to the dish.

Onion Rings

4 cups neutral oil, for frying

2 large sweet or yellow onions

⅓ cup cornstarch

1 cup all-purpose flour

½ cup panko breadcrumbs

2 teaspoons kosher salt

1 teaspoon baking powder

1 teaspoon onion powder

1 teaspoon seasoned salt, plus more for serving

1 cup whole milk

1 large egg

Zip Sauce

½ cup sour cream

1½ teaspoons ketchup

1½ teaspoons prepared horseradish

1 tablespoon fresh lemon juice

½ teaspoon sugar

¼ teaspoon cayenne pepper

¼ teaspoon dry mustard

¼ teaspoon seasoned salt

Make the onion rings: In a deep pot, heat the oil to 375°F over medium heat. Line a baking sheet with paper towels. Prepare an ice bath in a large bowl.

Cut the onions into ½-inch-thick slices and separate into rings. Transfer the rings to the ice water, let soak for 15 minutes, then remove them and pat them completely dry (this will help neutralize the sharp onion flavor). In a medium bowl, toss the rings with the cornstarch and set aside.

In a large bowl, mix the flour, breadcrumbs, kosher salt, baking powder, onion powder, and seasoned salt. In a small bowl, whisk the milk and egg together until well combined. Gradually pour the milk mixture into the flour mixture while whisking continuously until a smooth, thick batter is formed.

Working in batches, dip the onion rings into the batter until coated evenly, shake off any excess, and then carefully drop the rings into the oil.

Fry the onion rings a few at a time until golden brown, about 1 minute 30 seconds on each side. Use a slotted spoon or tongs to transfer the onion rings to the paper towels to drain. Sprinkle with seasoned salt. Repeat with the remaining onion rings.

Make the zip sauce: In a small bowl, mix together the sour cream, ketchup, horseradish, lemon juice, sugar, cayenne, dry mustard, and seasoned salt.

Serve the onion rings immediately with the zip sauce on the side.

PINEAPPLE GINGER DRINK

Makes about 5 cups

The sight of a pot of boiling tea and the aroma of fruit and herbs wafting from it was a common experience during my childhood. My mom would take ginger and pineapple peels and steep them together with dried fruits and herbs to get a second use out of ingredients. Those drinks were delicious and inspired me to make my own juice blends at home. This is my version that doesn't use trimmings, but it still reminds me of the flavors my mom put into those teas. I like mine chilled, not too sweet, with a good amount of lime and club soda, but how or when you enjoy this is completely up to you.

8 ounces fresh ginger, peeled

1½ pounds fresh pineapple, peeled, cored, and coarsely chopped

½ teaspoon kosher salt

4 cups hot water

Juice of 1 lime

1 cup honey, or to taste

Club soda, for serving (optional)

Use the flat part of a chef's knife or a heavy pot to smash the ginger.

In a blender, add the ginger, pineapple, salt, and 2 cups of water and blend on high until well incorporated. Pour through a fine-mesh sieve into a pitcher. Rinse the blender with ½ cup of water and add it to the pitcher. Stir in the 4 cups hot water and the lime juice. While it's still warm, sweeten the tea by whisking in the honey. The tea can be enjoyed hot, or chilled and served with club soda.

PALM WINE SANGRIA

Makes about 5 cups

This is a great party drink that highlights palm wine, a traditional alcoholic beverage from Ghana that is slightly floral, with a fermented tang to it. The wine is made from the sap of palm trees that is left to ferment for a few hours (or days), resulting in a uniquely sweet, cloudy beverage with a relatively low alcohol content. It's a great base for a sangria made with a ton of fruit and peach schnapps. Serve this punch over ice or in a big bowl at your next dinner party.

1 medium navel orange, sliced ⅛ inch thick, plus more orange slices for garnish

1 medium Granny Smith apple, cored and cut into ¼-inch dice

1 medium white peach, pitted and cut into ¼-inch dice

½ cup stemmed and ¼-inch-diced strawberries

3⅓ cups palm wine

½ cup peach schnapps

½ cup fresh lime juice

Fresh mint leaves, for garnish

In a ½ gallon mason jar fitted with a lid or in a standard pitcher, combine the orange, apple, peach, and strawberries. Add the palm wine, schnapps, and lime juice and stir to combine well. Refrigerate for at least 2 hours or up to 8 hours.

To serve, fill glasses with ice and top with sangria and some of the fruit. Garnish with orange slices and mint leaves.

WARM MALTED IRISH CREAM

Makes 1 cup

Milo is a chocolate malt drink that was first introduced to Ghana in the 1970s by Nestlé. Nowadays, it's almost impossible to walk through a mall or drive around the capital city without seeing an ad for Milo. Once, when I was in Washington, D.C., I had a conversation with chef Aisah Siraj from the Philippines about how big Milo is in both Ghana and the Philippines (Aisah laughed at me because of how I pronounced Milo with a short "i" versus how she pronounced it with a long "i.") We reminisced about drinking Milo as children, and realized that now that we're older and of legal age, we can enjoy a more adult version with the addition of sweet Irish cream. It's our (and our moms') preferred way of imbibing this iconic drink.

6 ounces whole milk

1 heaping tablespoon Milo, plus more for garnish

1 to 2 ounces Irish cream liqueur, to taste (I like Baileys or Amarula)

Organic store-bought canned whipped cream, for serving

Place the milk in a glass jar with a lid. Shake the jar until the milk is frothy, then uncover and microwave for 30 seconds to warm (see Note). In a mug, add the Milo, then the Irish cream. Pour in the frothed milk and mix until the cream and Milo are incorporated. Top with whipped cream, dust with more Milo, and serve.

Note: This recipe works just as well with warm milk that has not been frothed.

TAMARIND LIMEADE

Makes 9 cups

My first experiences with tamarind were when I lived in Ghana as a child. I remember both eating the fruit raw as a snack and having it in this drink. Seen all over the African diaspora and in Indian cuisine, tamarind is also used in condiments and savory dishes. For this juice, tamarind paste is soaked in water and then strained to create a tangy yet refreshing drink. It's sweetened with coconut palm sugar, a specialty sugar made from the sap of the coconut plant, which stands up to the tartness of tamarind. You can find tamarind paste at your local grocer and coconut palm sugar on Amazon or in Caribbean and Asian markets.

¾ cup chopped coconut palm sugar from a block

2 tablespoons tamarind paste

1 to 1¼ cups fresh lime juice

In a kettle or a small saucepan over medium-high heat, bring 1 cup of water to a boil. In a small bowl, combine the boiling water, sugar, and tamarind paste and stir until the sugar is dissolved.

Strain the tamarind mixture into a pitcher or large bowl. Stir in 1 cup of the lime juice and 7 cups of water. Taste and add the remaining lime juice if you prefer more tartness. To serve, pour into ice-filled glasses.

SOBOLO

Makes about 6½ cups This magenta-colored tea made from dehydrated hibiscus flowers is the signature drink that connects people of African descent around the world. It has so many other names: sorrel, zobolo, red drink, flor de Jamaica. It's kind of like curry, where you get a different recipe depending on where you're at in the world, and even from house to house. My take has warm spices like grains of Selim, cinnamon, and clove, which you would commonly see in Ghana. I love the punch of ginger, but you can use a little less if you'd like. Dried hibiscus is pretty easy to find at most supermarkets and grocery stores as loose-leaf tea.

1 navel orange, plus orange twists or slices for garnish

10 allspice berries

5 grains of Selim (for sourcing, see page 26)

4 star anise pods

2 cinnamon sticks

2 whole cloves

½ pineapple (about 1½ pounds), cut into ¼-inch chunks with the skin on

2 (5-inch) pieces of fresh ginger, peeled and coarsely grated

8 ounces dried hibiscus flowers (sorrel) or 8 ounces hibiscus tea bags

1½ cups sugar, or to taste

2 tablespoons fresh lime juice, or to taste

Using a vegetable peeler, remove wide strips of orange peel, then juice the orange, keeping the peel and juice separate. Set aside.

In a large stockpot over medium-high heat, combine the allspice, grains of Selim, star anise, cinnamon sticks, and cloves. Toast, stirring often, until fragrant, about 3 minutes. Add the pineapple, ginger, and orange peel. Cook, stirring, until the peel is fragrant, about 3 minutes. Add 7 cups of water and bring to a boil. Boil for 3 minutes. Add the hibiscus and turn off the heat. Cover the pot and let steep for at least 30 minutes or up to 1 hour.

Set a fine-mesh sieve over a large bowl and pour the hibiscus mixture through. Press on the solids to extract as much liquid as possible, then discard the solids. Add the reserved orange juice, the sugar, and lime juice and stir until the sugar is dissolved. Taste and adjust with more sugar or lime juice if desired. Cover and refrigerate until completely cool, at least 2 hours. The sobolo will keep in an airtight container in the refrigerator for 2 weeks.

To serve, pour into glasses or a punch bowl filled with ice and garnish with orange slices.

IN MEMORY OF
JOHN SWANZY,
GOVERNOR OF ACCRA, & MEMBER OF COUNCIL,
6TH SON OF HENRY & ANNE SWANZY,
OF AVELREAGH CO MONACHAN, IRELAND,
WHO DIED AT CAPE COAST CASTLE 22ND OCTR 1807

HIS LAST ACT WAS TO SAVE FROM SLAVERY
SOME OF THE FANTEES, SEIZED AFTER THE
CAPITULATION OF FORT ANNAMABOE TO THE
KING OF ASHANTEE.

SOUPS AND STEWS

Returning to Ghana:
A Turning Point

The greeting of humidity as I deplaned at Kotoka Airport in Accra is one of the first memories of the trip I took there in 2011, a pivotal visit that cemented my desire to tell my story.

If you've ever been to Africa or the Caribbean or anywhere with a hot climate, you know that as soon as the plane cabin doors open, the heat and humidity hit you, announcing you're in a new location. I was in graduate school at the time in London, studying for a master's degree in international public health nutrition at the University of Westminster, and had finally saved up enough money to buy a ticket to visit Ghana. I was there to work on a thesis about Maggi seasoning cubes (or bouillon cubes), and how they were becoming a bigger part of African cooking. But I was also there to pay my respects to two important people in my family's burial plot: my grandmother and my father, who was buried in Kumasi in 2005. I had gone to his wake and service in the United States but wasn't able to attend his burial, so this felt like it would offer me some closure.

I spent the first couple of weeks in Accra with my aunt Vivian, uncle Richard, and their sons, Isaac, Richmond, and Boakye. Richmond took me to Makola Market to start collecting information for my thesis. He was a buffer, translating conversations and acting as my tour guide, because while I can understand Twi, if someone's speaking fast, things still kind of go over my head.

For three days I interviewed home cooks for my thesis and ate as much as I could, trying to soak up as much of Ghana as possible—as though taking the culture into my blood via my taste buds. A typical day of eating looked like this: for breakfast I ate sugar bread, a staple of the Ghanaian diet, with eggs and tea or Milo chocolate drink. For lunch and dinner, I ate a lot of kenkey and banku, starchy grapefruit-size balls of steamed fermented cornmeal and cassava served with Ghanaian stews and fried fish. I ate rice balls and fufu. I ate a lot of fried and grilled tilapia. And so much shito. Grilled lamb or beef chichinga were a great snack, bought on the street while I was walking around, and eaten while soaking up as many of the sounds and the sights as I could. My time with my father and the many meals we had shared weighed heavy on my mind during my trip. Family loomed large, especially when I arrived in Kumasi.

My grandmother, Madame Ama Konamaah, was seventy-two years old when she passed away and was a pillar of the community in Kumasi. Her funeral was intense. Not only because it was hard to watch my mom and my aunt say goodbye to their mother, but also because members of the community who had known my grandmother wanted to pay their respects as well. At her home in Kumasi, the same one that I had spent time in as a child, my family was able to reconnect and unplug away from our day-to-day lives. It made us closer for sure.

When it was finally time to visit my father's grave, we loaded up our family in the car and drove to the burial site. When I saw his final resting place in Ghana, all

I could say to him over and over again was "I'm sorry." The image will stay with me forever: the lettering of his name, Benjamin Akwasi Adjepong, was slightly faded due to years of sun exposure. Saying goodbye to my grandmother and father with my extended family—my mom, stepfather, brother, cousins, aunt, paternal grandmother, and father's brother, Kojo—was extremely emotional. I was sorry I'd let a grudge keep me from speaking to him the last few months of his life. I wanted the grounds of the site to be better kept. I wanted to see beautiful flowers and landscaping, not this sun-bleached yard in front of the cement company that had bought the land nearby a few years after his burial. I cried as I thought about our time together in New York during my childhood, how he showed me the world through food, and how much I missed him. And then a sense of settling, of having some closure from acknowledging a wound that had remained unhealed for so long, overcame me as I looked at the faces around me. I noticed how my uncle Kojo looks just like me, and seeing him next to his mother, I could see where my father's features came from, features that got passed down to me. My past was present in their faces.

Even though I hadn't seen these family members in a long time, and I'd spent most of my life across the Atlantic in America, I was still connected to them through grief and bloodlines. I felt loved and held by my family at that moment. Going back to Ghana at that time was pivotal because it showed me that I can always depend on my family and that foundation. I know that if I had nothing left, not a single dollar to my name, I could survive in America and Africa because my family is my support system.

That experience helped shape how I am as a father to my daughter and how I talk to everyone I meet. I always encourage people to ask their parents about their childhoods and their history because there's so much more I wish I knew about my dad as a person. I recently saw photos of him as a teen, and it made me think of all of the questions I would ask him if I were able to take another cab ride with him today:

"What did you like to do when you were a teenager?"

"What fears do you have about the future?"

"What regrets do you have about the past?"

"What happened with my mom?"

Those unanswered questions are always the hardest to settle in your spirit. There are many more meals I wish we could have had together. But the memories of us eating in his taxi, spending time as father and son over food that opened up a world of flavors for me, will never leave me. Those formative experiences with my father impacted how I see the world and how I combine the Ghanaian flavors I grew up eating with flavors I'm introduced to in my travels all over the world. I'll never stop exploring and experimenting, thanks to my father.

WAAKYE STEW

Serves 4 to 6

In West African cuisine, red sauce made with tomatoes, peppers, ginger, and onions is a mother sauce, like tomato sauce in Italy or mole in Mexico. Waakye is a dish featuring rice, red peas, and a variation of that red stew-y sauce. It's traditionally made with cow offal and shrimp powder, which results in a red sauce that's darker in color and has more tangy depth of flavor with the inclusion of clove and anise seed. These strongly flavored ingredients all work together because waakye itself is a busy dish. Along with the spiced sauce and meat, there are fried elements, and it's typically served with rice, gari (granulated cassava), spaghetti, and sometimes even an egg. If you have all of those components, you want your stew sauce to be able to stand up to them.

Black Pepper–Clove Blend

1 tablespoon whole black peppercorns

1 teaspoon ground cloves

Meat

½ pound offal of your choice (I like cow foot or skin), cut into cubes the same size as the meat (optional)

1 medium Spanish onion, coarsely chopped

3 garlic cloves

1 (thumb-size) piece of fresh ginger, peeled and coarsely chopped

2 Maggi seasoning cubes, crushed (for sourcing, see page 31)

¼ teaspoon cumin seeds

¼ teaspoon dried rosemary

¼ teaspoon anise seeds

1 pound goat stew meat or beef stew meat, cut into small cubes

Neutral oil, for frying

Stew

2 pounds (5 or 6 medium) Roma tomatoes, cored and coarsely chopped

3 orange Scotch bonnet peppers or habanero peppers, to taste (optional)

4 medium Spanish onions, 3 coarsely chopped, 1 halved and thinly sliced through its core

2 (thumb-size) pieces of fresh ginger, peeled and coarsely chopped

5 garlic cloves

½ cup neutral oil

¾ cup tomato paste

1 tablespoon curry powder, homemade (page 39) or store-bought

1 teaspoon anise seeds

½ teaspoon ground cloves

2 fresh bay leaves

2 Maggi seasoning cubes, crushed (for sourcing, see page 31)

2 tablespoons shrimp powder (such as Badia brand)

1 tablespoon dried fish powder (such as stockfish powder)

2 teaspoons kosher salt

Gari

1 cup gari (for sourcing, see page 26)

3 tablespoons hot water

Kosher salt

Waakye Rice, for serving (page 167)

Make the black pepper–clove blend: Using a spice grinder, grind the peppercorns, then mix together with the cloves until well combined. This will season both the meat and stew. Set aside.

Prepare the meat: Rinse the offal well under cool water, if using. In a blender or food processor, blend the onion, garlic, ginger, Maggi cubes, cumin seeds, rosemary, anise seeds, and 2 cups of water until smooth.

In a large pot, combine the offal and goat and pour the onion mixture over. Stir well, then place the pot over medium-high heat. Add 1 tablespoon of the black pepper–clove blend. Cover the pot, leaving the lid slightly cracked for ventilation.

Recipe continues

Let it cook for 15 to 20 minutes over medium-high heat, until the impurities from the offal and goat come up to the top. Reduce the heat to a simmer and steam the meat until tender, 25 to 30 minutes. Remove the meat and offal from the pot and set aside on a plate. Strain and reserve the meat broth. You should have about 4 cups; if needed, add more water to equal 4 cups. Set aside.

In a medium pot, add enough oil to come ¼ inch up the side of the pot. Heat over medium heat. Line a plate with paper towels. When the oil shimmers, pat the meat and offal dry and fry in batches, turning often, until deep golden all over, 8 to 10 minutes, then set aside on the paper towels to drain any excess oil.

Make the stew: In a blender or food processor, blend the tomatoes and Scotch bonnet peppers (if using) until smooth and place in a small pot. Set over medium-high heat and bring to a simmer. Cook, stirring frequently, until the sauce is reduced to about 3 cups and the raw flavor is cooked out, about 20 minutes. Set aside. (See Note.)

In a blender or food processor, blend the 3 chopped onions, ginger, and garlic with 1 cup of water until smooth. Heat the oil in a large heavy-bottomed pot over medium-high heat, then add the sliced onion. Cook, stirring often, until translucent, about 2 minutes. Add the blended onion mixture and continue to cook, stirring frequently, until the liquid has evaporated and the mixture is very thick and just beginning to caramelize, about 20 minutes. Add the cooked tomato sauce, tomato paste, curry powder, anise seeds, cloves, bay leaves, and Maggi cubes. Stir well to combine and reduce the heat to medium.

Cover the pot, leaving the lid cracked for ventilation, and cook, stirring frequently, until the oil begins to separate and rise to the top, 30 to 40 minutes. You want this sauce to be thick. Add 2 cups of the reserved meat broth, the meat and offal, shrimp powder, dried fish powder, and remaining black pepper–clove blend. (Leftover meat broth will keep in an airtight container in the fridge for up to 4 days or in the freezer for 3 months.) Reduce the heat to medium-low and simmer gently, uncovered and stirring occasionally, to allow the flavors to meld, about 15 minutes. Remove excess oil by skimming with a spoon or ladle. Season with the salt and more spices, if desired. Remove the bay leaves.

Just before serving, make the gari: In a large bowl, mix the gari, hot water, and 2 or 3 tablespoons of the waakye stew (enough to cover the gari) with a spoon until well combined. Season with salt to taste. Sprinkle the gari over the stew and serve.

Waakye stew will keep in an airtight container in the refrigerator for 1 week.

Note: You can also use 3 cups of canned tomato sauce and skip the process of making your own tomato sauce.

FANTE FANTE FISH STEW

Serves 4

When I was growing up, my mom would often make fish stew. Even to this day, fish stew is one of the go-to dishes that she can whip up fairly quickly and adapt easily. I think of it like a fisherman's stew that uses a lot of pantry items, but every ingredient matters in this dish. My recipe stays pretty close to the traditional version with palm oil and shrimp powder to give it an earthiness and spice. You can use clams, mussels, or really any fresh fish or shellfish you like in this dish—but the key is that the seafood is fresh. I'd serve it with a big plate of rice or banku.

Spice Blend

5 whole cloves

1 calabash nutmeg (for sourcing, see page 25)

3 grains of Selim (for sourcing, see page 26)

½ teaspoon anise seeds

¼ teaspoon grains of paradise

1 tablespoon All-Day Seasoning Blend (page 35)

Marinade

1 large white onion

1 cup green kpakpo shito peppers, stemmed

2 garlic cloves

1 (thumb-size) piece of fresh ginger, peeled and coarsely chopped

2 (3 to 4 pounds each) whole red snapper, scaled, gutted, and cut into ½-inch-thick steaks (heads and tails are okay; see Notes, page 98)

Kosher salt

Stew

Avocado oil

Kosher salt

¼ cup virgin coconut oil

½ cup red palm oil (see Notes, page 98)

1 large Spanish onion, halved and sliced

1 (28-ounce) can crushed tomatoes

¼ cup shrimp powder (for sourcing, see page 25)

2 tablespoons curry powder, homemade (page 39) or store-bought

Cooked white rice, or a swallow such as fufu (page 176) or banku (page 173), for serving

Make the spice blend: In a small skillet over low heat, toast the cloves, nutmeg, grains of Selim, anise seeds, grains of paradise, and seasoning blend, swirling often to toast evenly, until fragrant, 2 to 3 minutes. Use a wooden spoon to mix the ingredients until well combined, then transfer to a small bowl.

Make the marinade: In a blender or food processor, combine the white onion, peppers, garlic, ginger, and all of the spice blend and blend until completely smooth. You should have about 2 cups of marinade.

Pat the fish dry with paper towels and place in a large bowl. Season all over with salt, then add ¼ cup of the marinade (reserve the rest for the stew). Cover with plastic wrap and marinate in the refrigerator for 4 to 8 hours.

Make the stew: In a large, deep sauté pan, add enough avocado oil to come 1½ inches up the side of the pan. Heat over medium-high heat until shimmering. Line a plate with paper towels.

Recipe continues

Remove the fish from the marinade and pat dry to remove excess moisture. Lightly season the fish with salt. Working in batches as necessary, fry the fish until golden (it will finish cooking in the stew), turning gently halfway through, 5 to 7 minutes. Transfer to the prepared plate and set aside. Repeat with the remaining fish, adding more oil if necessary in between batches.

Discard the oil and heat the same pan over medium-high heat. When the pan is hot, add the coconut and palm oils. When the oil shimmers, add the Spanish onion. Sauté, stirring often, until translucent, 3 to 5 minutes, then add the remaining marinade. Cook, stirring frequently, until fragrant and somewhat reduced, about 5 minutes. Add the crushed tomatoes, season with salt, and stir to combine. Reduce the heat to low and simmer until well combined, about 10 minutes. Taste and adjust the salt. Add the shrimp powder, curry powder, and fried fish. Stir gently and cover the pan. Simmer until the fish is cooked through, 10 to 12 minutes.

Serve over rice or with a swallow. The stew will keep in an airtight container in the refrigerator for up to 10 days.

Notes: Your fishmonger should be able to prep the fish for you. Ask to have the fish scaled and gutted, then cut into steaks, leaving the head and tail on.

Take the time to find sustainably sourced red palm oil. I prefer Royal Palm red palm oil, which can be found online or at your local African market.

NKATE NKWAN NE AKƆMFƐM
Groundnut Soup with Guinea Fowl

Serves 4 to 6

Groundnuts have been an integral part of many African cuisines for centuries, and this dish is one that has stood the test of time. It's probably the first savory dish I can remember eating as a child. Made with groundnut paste and tomatoes, it's earthy, spicy, and slightly sweet. My mother would make big batches of it to keep in the freezer, so it was a staple when I was growing up—an easy meal she could defrost and have on the table quickly, served with steamed rice or fufu. Groundnut soup translates to comfort for me and for so many other West African kids. I use peanut butter in place of the groundnut paste when I make this in the States. If you're unable to find guinea fowl, you may substitute chicken, and it will be just as heartwarming.

Marinade

1 large yellow onion, coarsely chopped

¼ cup peeled and coarsely chopped fresh ginger

¼ cup garlic cloves, crushed

5 Maggi seasoning cubes (for sourcing, see page 31)

2½ teaspoons anise seeds

2 teaspoons Mom's Hot Pepper Sauce (page 43) or store-bought Scotch bonnet hot sauce

1 (2-pound) guinea fowl, cut into 8 pieces, or 2 pounds guinea fowl drumsticks

1 tablespoon kosher salt

2 teaspoons sweet paprika

Groundnut Paste

1½ cups unsalted natural creamy peanut butter or groundnut paste

3½ tablespoons tomato paste

Soup

2 tablespoons avocado oil

3 cups reduced-sodium chicken stock or vegetable stock

1 small yellow onion, quartered

2 small Roma tomatoes

2 habanero peppers

1 (15-ounce) can tomato sauce

Swallow such as banku (page 173) or fufu (page 176) or cooked white rice, for serving

Make the marinade: In a blender or food processor, blend the onion, ginger, garlic, Maggi cubes, anise seeds, and hot pepper sauce until a smooth paste forms. In a medium bowl, season the guinea fowl all over with the salt and paprika, then add the onion mixture. Cover and refrigerate for 4 to 8 hours.

While the guinea fowl marinates, make the groundnut paste: In a large nonstick pan, combine the peanut butter and tomato paste and cook over medium heat, stirring often, until a dry, thick orangish paste forms, 3 to 5 minutes. You should have a scant 2 cups of paste. Set aside.

Remove the guinea fowl from the refrigerator to come to room temperature. When ready to cook, remove the guinea fowl from the marinade and pat dry, removing as much marinade as possible and reserving it.

Make the soup: In a large pot over medium heat, heat the avocado oil. When the oil is shimmering, add the guinea fowl and sear, working in batches if necessary, until deeply browned all over, about 2 minutes per side. When all the meat has been browned, return it to the pot, add the reserved marinade, and stir to coat. Reduce the heat to low and cook gently, stirring often, until the marinade is reduced and caramelized, 12 to 15 minutes.

Recipe continues

Gradually add the chicken stock, stirring to deglaze the pot, followed by the onion, tomatoes, and habaneros. Return to a gentle simmer over medium heat and cook until the tomatoes and onion are soft, 10 minutes. Remove the pot from the heat. Use a slotted spoon to transfer the onion, tomatoes, and habaneros to a blender, add the tomato sauce, and blend until smooth. Return the pot to the heat and add the blended mixture along with the groundnut paste. Stir thoroughly until fully incorporated. Simmer gently until peanut oil rises to the surface of the stew, 10 to 15 minutes, adjusting the heat as necessary to keep from scorching or spattering.

Serve hot with a swallow or white rice.

SWEET POTATO PEANUT STEW

Serves 4 to 6

Like many others during the early months of 2020, I had a plan for what I wanted the year to look like. For months I had been working diligently on opening my first quick-service restaurant in Washington, D.C., called On The Double, where the menu would be a mash-up of West African and Caribbean food. This sweet potato peanut stew was a vegetarian offering from the menu. Filling, well spiced, and naturally sweet, it's comfort in a bowl, offering a taste of the Caribbean in a hearty, meat-free way. Because of the Covid-19 lockdown, On The Double never opened, but one of my favorite quotes from that year was that "adversity is a terrible thing to waste." So I held on to this recipe and repurposed it. I started teaching the recipe in online cooking classes that year, gaining more meaningful connections worldwide than I ever would have in D.C.

1 tablespoon high-quality extra-virgin olive oil

1 medium yellow onion, diced

1 tablespoon tomato paste

3 garlic cloves, minced

1 (½-inch) piece of fresh ginger, peeled and minced

2 teaspoons ground cumin

1 teaspoon ground coriander

4 cups reduced-sodium vegetable stock

1 (14.5-ounce) can crushed tomatoes

2 medium sweet potatoes, peeled and cut into medium dice

1 tablespoon curry powder, homemade (page 39) or store-bought

1 teaspoon Mom's Hot Pepper Sauce (page 43) or store-bought Scotch bonnet hot sauce, or more to taste

1 teaspoon kosher salt, plus more to taste

¾ cup unsalted natural creamy peanut butter

4 cups (packed) fresh baby spinach

Coconut Rice (page 151) or white rice, for serving

1 tablespoon coarsely chopped roasted peanuts, for garnish

Set a medium Dutch oven over medium-low heat. When it's hot, add the olive oil and onion. Cook, stirring occasionally, until softened, 6 to 8 minutes. Add the tomato paste, garlic, ginger, cumin, and coriander and cook, stirring frequently, to get some color on the tomato paste, an additional minute.

Add the stock, crushed tomatoes, sweet potatoes, curry powder, hot pepper sauce, and salt. Raise the heat to high and bring to a boil. Reduce the heat to low and simmer, uncovered, until the sweet potatoes are soft, about 10 minutes. Stir in the peanut butter and then the spinach and cook until the peanut butter is well incorporated and the spinach has wilted, about 2 minutes. Taste and adjust the salt and spice level, if desired. Serve hot with coconut or white rice, garnished with peanuts.

CHICKEN
with Light Soup

Serves 4 to 6

Older chickens, or stewing hens, get a bad rap for being tough or gamey. But if you braise an older chicken in a soup or stew just right, it becomes so tender and delicious. I suggest for this recipe that you ask your butcher for a stewing hen or guinea fowl because braising a standard chicken might result in meat that becomes too mushy, or even shreds, before the soup is finished cooking. Every Ghanaian household has its own recipe for light soup, also known as pepper soup, adding more or fewer peppers or swapping out the poultry for another protein. It's the go-to comfort soup, similar to chicken noodle or any other soup you'd have if you're not feeling too well (the spices and ginger can also help with any congestion). Freeze it and keep it around for an easy dinner.

Marinade

1 (3-pound) stewing chicken or guinea hen, cut into 8 pieces

1 heaping tablespoon tomato paste

2 dried bay leaves

1 large red onion, coarsely chopped

2 Scotch bonnet peppers, stemmed and seeded (see Notes)

1 tablespoon fresh rosemary leaves

Leaves from 2 sprigs of thyme

4 garlic cloves

1 (thumb-size) piece of fresh ginger, peeled and coarsely chopped

2 teaspoons kosher salt

1 teaspoon ground cumin

½ teaspoon anise seeds

¼ teaspoon black peppercorns

3 grains of Selim (for sourcing, see page 26)

Soup

1 medium red onion, left whole

3 medium very ripe Roma tomatoes

3 garden eggs (for sourcing, see page 26), 2 stemmed and left whole, 1 sliced lengthwise into ½-inch-thick slices (optional; see Notes)

1 medium carrot, coarsely chopped

2 star anise pods

2 Maggi seasoning cubes (for sourcing, see page 31)

5 medium okra pods (optional)

2 Scotch bonnet peppers, left whole (optional)

1 sprig of fresh basil

Kosher salt

Fufu (page 176) or cooked white rice, for serving

Make the marinade: Place the chicken pieces on a baking sheet and remove any skin from the breast and dark meat, keeping the wings intact. (If there are any feathers on the wing, use an open flame to singe them off.) Transfer the chicken to a large pot and add the tomato paste and bay leaves. Set aside.

In a blender, combine the chopped onion, Scotch bonnets, rosemary, thyme, garlic, ginger, salt, cumin, anise seeds, peppercorns, and grains of Selim. Blend into a smooth paste, adding just enough water so that it combines (start with ¼ cup and add 1 tablespoon at a time as needed). Pour the marinade over the chicken. Rinse the blender with ½ cup of water and pour over the chicken, stirring to coat the chicken thoroughly in the marinade. Cover and marinate at room temperature for 1 hour (or transfer to the refrigerator and marinate for up to 1 day).

Make the soup: Cut small slits in the whole onion, tomatoes, and whole garden eggs (if using), then place in a medium pot with the carrot, star anise, Maggi cubes, and 8 cups of water. Place over medium heat. At the same time, put the pot of chicken on the stove, covered, over medium heat. Cook both pots for about 25 minutes, stirring the chicken occasionally just until the marinade starts to thicken, the oils separate, and the chicken starts to release its own juices. After 25 minutes, continue to cook the chicken (still stirring occasionally and scraping down the sides of the pot), but remove the pot of whole vegetables from the stove; they should be extremely tender at this point. Remove the star anise from the pot and reserve the water. Using a slotted spoon, add the whole vegetables to a blender and blend on high until well combined. After about 40 minutes of cooking the chicken, place a strainer over the pot of chicken and pour the blended vegetables through the strainer, straining out any roughage. Pour the water that was used to cook the whole vegetables through the strainer and mix well. Now that everything is in one pot, simmer the chicken for an additional 30 minutes, or until the oils start to rise to the top of the soup. Skim off any impurities, then add the okra (if using), sliced garden egg (if using), whole Scotch bonnets (if you're looking for more heat), and basil. Turn the soup to low and cook for 15 minutes, or just until the vegetables are soft.

Remove the whole Scotch bonnets and bay leaves and season the soup with salt. Serve immediately with fufu or white rice. The soup will keep in an airtight container in the refrigerator for up to 1 week.

Notes: If you're looking for more heat, use the whole Scotch bonnet peppers in the marinade.

You can substitute each garden egg with ¼ Japanese eggplant, sliced ½ inch thick.

CURRIED CORN BISQUE
with Salmon

Serves 6

This dish is important to me because it is the first recipe I created after culinary school. It was also the dish I cooked for the casting producers on *Top Chef* in 2017, which eventually led me to being cast for the show. In-season corn is sweet and juicy and pairs perfectly with curry, a flavor I love incorporating into dishes. The spice blend complements, rather than overtakes, the flavor of fresh corn. At this point, I've made this recipe what feels like thousands of times, but the process is always exciting to me.

Bisque

2 tablespoons neutral oil

1 cup diced shallots

6 to 8 garlic cloves, coarsely chopped

4 cups reduced-sodium chicken stock

5 cups fresh corn kernels

5 tablespoons unsalted butter

3 to 5 tablespoons curry powder, homemade (page 39) or store-bought

2 teaspoons kosher salt, plus more to taste

1 small bunch thyme

1 cup whole milk

½ cup heavy cream

Salmon

6 (3- to 4-ounce) salmon fillets, skin on

Kosher salt

2 tablespoons grapeseed or avocado oil

3 sprigs of thyme

1 head garlic, cut in half crosswise

1 tablespoon unsalted butter

Make the bisque: In a medium pot over medium-low heat, heat the neutral oil until it shimmers. Add the shallots and chopped garlic and cook, stirring, until tender, 4 to 6 minutes. Meanwhile, in a small pot over high heat, heat the chicken stock just until it reaches a simmer.

Add the corn kernels to the shallot mixture and cook until tender and bright yellow, about 5 minutes. Add the butter, stir until melted, then remove from the heat.

Transfer the corn mixture and warm stock to a high-speed blender and blend until completely smooth. (Be sure to blend using a cover to prevent any spattering of hot liquid, and leave the lid cracked to let steam escape. Work in batches if necessary.) Rinse the medium pot, then strain the soup through a fine-mesh sieve into the clean pot. Heat gently over medium-low heat until the soup comes to a slow simmer, 3 to 5 minutes. Whisk in the curry powder (start with 3 tablespoons) and salt. Add the thyme bunch and reduce the heat to low. Steep the thyme in the soup for 20 minutes. Meanwhile, heat the milk and cream in a separate small pot over low heat just until warmed through.

Strain the soup once more through the fine-mesh sieve, then stir in the warm cream mixture. Taste and adjust the seasoning with more curry powder and salt if desired, then cover and keep warm. Warm 6 soup bowls.

Recipe continues

Make the salmon: Pat the salmon very dry with paper towels and season all over with salt.

In a 12-inch nonstick or cast-iron skillet over medium-high heat, heat the grapeseed oil until hot and shimmering. Add the salmon skin-side down and cook, without moving, until golden and crisp, about 2 minutes. Carefully flip the fillets and reduce the heat to medium. Add the thyme sprigs, garlic head, and butter to the pan around the fillets. While basting with butter, continue to cook the salmon to your liking, about 4 minutes more for medium-rare and 6 minutes more for medium.

In the center of each warmed bowl, add 1 salmon fillet and slowly pour hot soup around the fillet. Serve right away.

ABENKWAN
Palm Nut Soup

Like many immigrant communities, West Africans have modified and adapted traditional dishes to what's available to them in their new homelands. Palm nut soup is traditionally made with the fruit of palm trees, which is easily found fresh in West and Central Africa, but in other places, canned palm nut cream is used. Though it can be very oily, it has a great rich and nutty flavor. I prefer to use Praise brand palm nut cream, which is found readily online. This slightly sweet and tangy creamy soup is especially popular in the Ashanti region of Ghana, where my family is from. Goat meat and guinea fowl are the proteins of choice, but you can use what you have available, such as beef, seafood, and smoked meats, or even just make it vegetarian. I like a little heat in my palm nut soup, but the spice level is up to you.

There are a couple of specialty ingredients in this recipe, like prekese, a tropical plant native to West Africa that gives the soup a uniquely sweet and smoky taste, as well as turkey berries, a mildly bitter and tangy nightshade found throughout the region. You can find turkey berries at your local African market sold fresh or canned—either version will work for this recipe. Serve with banku or with boiled yams.

3 grains of Selim (for sourcing, see page 26)

½ teaspoon anise seeds

1 prekese pod (for sourcing, see page 32)

Marinade

1¼ pounds goat stew meat

8 ounces guinea fowl or smoked turkey neck, cut into 8 pieces

2½ tablespoons kosher salt

2 medium red onions, coarsely chopped

4 garlic cloves

2 (thumb-size) pieces of fresh ginger, peeled and coarsely chopped

1 serrano chili, stemmed and coarsely chopped

½ Scotch bonnet pepper, stemmed and seeded (keep the seeds for more heat)

5 Maggi seasoning cubes (for sourcing, see page 31)

Soup

3 Roma tomatoes

4 ounces superku (salted cod), soaked overnight and rinsed before using (optional)

½ cup turkey berries (preferably fresh but canned is okay)

1¼ cups palm nut cream concentrate

Boiling water, as needed

5 ounces fresh okra and/ or fresh white garden eggs (for sourcing, see page 26), stemmed and cut into ¼-inch slices (optional)

Cooked white rice or a swallow such as banku (page 173) or fufu (page 176), for serving

In a small pan over medium heat, toast the grains of Selim, anise seeds, and prekese until fragrant, 3 to 5 minutes. Leave in the pan and set aside.

Make the marinade: In a medium pot, combine the goat meat and guinea fowl. Season with the salt.

In a blender, combine the onions, garlic, ginger, serrano, Scotch bonnet, Maggi cubes, and the toasted anise seeds and grains of Selim (reserve the toasted prekese for the soup). Pulse into a puree, adding a few tablespoons of water to get the

Recipe continues

blender going, if needed. Pour the marinade over the goat meat and guinea fowl, then cover and transfer to the refrigerator to marinate for at least 2 hours or up to 2 days.

Make the soup: Take the pot out of the refrigerator and set over medium-high heat. Add enough water to just submerge the meat, then add the whole tomatoes and cook until the skin of the tomatoes begins to peel back, skimming off any impurities that rise to the surface, about 15 minutes. Once the tomato peels begin to separate, remove the tomatoes from the pot and peel away and discard the skins. Set the tomatoes aside.

Add the toasted prekese and superku (if using) to the pot, stirring gently to combine. Bring to a boil over high heat, then reduce the heat to medium-high and simmer until fragrant, another 15 minutes.

In a blender, combine the peeled tomatoes and turkey berries and blend to a smooth paste, adding a little water if necessary to help the machine. Strain through a fine-mesh sieve, discarding the solids, and add the liquid to the simmering pot.

Meanwhile, in a large bowl, add the palm nut cream and enough boiling water to just submerge. Whisk until smooth. Set aside to allow any sediment to settle at the bottom, about 15 minutes. Stir the palm nut liquid into the soup. Cook, using a large spoon to skim off any impurities and excess oil that rise to the top, until the top of the simmering soup is clear of oil, about 20 minutes. Add the sliced okra (if using) and cook until it is just tender, about 10 minutes. (If using garden egg, slice it in half and score the flesh. Cover with salt and set aside for 15 minutes. Rinse the salt off under cold water, pat dry, and add to the soup with the okra.)

Serve immediately with white rice or a swallow.

SALADS AND VEGETABLES

Woforo Dua Pa a, or Learning to Climb the Tree

There's a time in everyone's life when you're a newbie at a skill, a job, or a craft, but you want to be further along. You might have the vision, but you don't have the execution quite yet or understand the landscape that you're stepping into. That time for me was when I was a line cook at Marc Forgione and at Rouge Tomate in Manhattan's Chelsea neighborhood. I had just graduated from Johnson & Wales University's culinary program in Providence, Rhode Island, my mind filled with delusions of grandeur, a rookie who thought my culinary school degree and confidence meant I should be a sous chef and have a managerial position in a professional kitchen immediately. I would actually come in to work and do my prep while thinking, "I deserve to be a sous chef or executive chef." I laugh at myself now because I see how cocky I was. I was living in a space of potential instead of reality, not seeing that I was at the base of a tree and had to start climbing. I hadn't yet put in the years it takes to become a great chef. I had so much unfounded bravado.

There are few environments more humbling than a professional restaurant kitchen. Everyone (or at least anyone who is any good) is working as hard as they can to do their job at the highest level possible, as quickly as possible, so it creates a sink-or-swim mentality. I really got my ass handed to me more than a few times, but I needed that in my career then. Working the line during a really busy dinner shift and falling behind, or messing up prep from earlier in the day, taught me valuable on-the-job skills that I combined with techniques and lessons learned in culinary school.

"How much more do you want to put in?"

This is a question I had to ask myself during this time. While I was working as a line cook, I was staying on Baychester Avenue in the Bronx, commuting to work downtown, and learning every day how to best accomplish a task or a set of tasks to put up the finest plate of food possible. But on the train, after work or before a shift, I had time to think and to ask myself where I was headed with my career and what I wanted out of my life.

Taking the train back and forth for shifts was grueling. It took one and a half hours each way on the 5, so to get to work at 12 p.m., I'd have to leave home at 10:15 a.m. That may not sound early, but it feels like it if you worked late the night before and regularly didn't get home until three or four in the morning like I did. And late at night, the trains never ran on time. I remember standing on the subway platform exhausted, waiting for the train, smelling like the food I'd spent all night cooking. I just wanted to get home and get to bed as soon as possible, but I had to wait. (And wait. And wait…)

As with many of the lessons in my life, I now know that there's an adinkra symbol that speaks to what I was feeling: "Woforo Dua Pa a," a reciprocal line drawing that looks a bit like two digital threes facing one another, which translates to "when you climb a good tree, you are given a push." The tree symbolizes the support you're given in working toward a good goal, giving you strength to see your dreams through. Building my skills and my knowledge while working as a line cook was like climbing a sturdy tree. I had to start at the bottom and work my way up, learning as I went along.

One of the biggest things I needed to learn was timing. In a professional kitchen, timing is everything, and I was blessed to learn that early on in my line cook days. At first, I sucked at it. When you're working the line at a restaurant and it's busy, you have to ensure that everything you're cooking is reaching its optimal temperature, texture, and flavor at the same time and that you're putting it on the plate fast enough so it doesn't lose any of those elements. On top of that, you have to make sure you're in sync with the rest of your team so the other plates that are going to the same table are all coming up at the same time. It's like a synchronized swimming routine or a basketball team passing a ball back and forth down the court to make a winning basket. And you have to keep in mind what's coming up next, since you're working multiple tickets at a time. Your chef is your coach, managing a team of cooks through each push, and each person on the line is playing a different position, so if you don't do your part, the team doesn't work well. It's a constant setting and resetting of ingredients, with back-to-back plays throughout the service, until each ticket is done, you clean the kitchen, and go home for the night.

When I worked at Marc Forgione, a restaurant that highlighted Italian and local seasonal produce, I knew coming into it that I had a bit of technique under my belt and I would learn skills that would take my cooking to the next level. But I hadn't thought about the countless hours I would spend on the line doing the actual work, prepping ingredients, and standing on my feet for long shifts that would leave me tired and aching. I lived in a space where I put more importance on the rewards for the work rather than actually doing it. The brigade system, used in formal fine-dining kitchens with a chef at the top and line cooks underneath, taught me that the work was going to be the point. It humbled me very quickly.

The kitchen was tiny, and my garde manger station (cold appetizers) had many components. When I came in to work, I had to prep ingredients that had varying cooking times: flatbread crackers that had to be baked in the oven but could not be too brown, pot roast braised until it was tender (which took many hours), and several soft-boiled eggs cooked and ready to go at any time for a salad. It took me many shifts to learn how to make those dishes in the proper order so that each one would be ready to go by service time. The only way a line cook can learn and succeed is by doing and experiencing the tasks firsthand.

Years later, when I finally did become a sous chef, I was grateful for those early days because I could see where the line cooks were coming from. I could understand the new kids because I had been there. I now know that was just the first branch along the tree for me to climb, and there would be many more to come.

GRILLED CORN
with Garlic Piri Piri Butter

Serves 4

Street vendors are the backbone of food culture in West Africa. No matter where in Ghana you go, there's almost always the aroma of charcoal and roasted corn coming from any cluster of vendors. Corn is relatively inexpensive and filling, which is why you'll see most vendors selling it as a side along with their mainstays, or a vendor selling corn and only corn. This recipe is inspired by those artisans, who grill corn with butter, garlic, spices, or a combination of all three.

4 ears of corn, husks removed

½ cup (1 stick) unsalted butter, at room temperature

2 garlic cloves, finely minced

1 tablespoon Piri Piri Rub (page 39)

⅛ teaspoon kosher salt

Preheat a gas or charcoal outdoor grill to high heat.

Fill a large bowl with water and soak the corn for 15 minutes. Drain and pat dry.

In a small bowl, mix together the butter, garlic, piri piri rub, and salt. Slather half of the piri piri butter on the corn.

Grill the corn until browned on all sides, rotating every 3 minutes, about 10 minutes total. Transfer to a serving platter and slather the remaining piri piri butter on the corn. Serve immediately.

ABUROO AND FONIO SALAD
with Honey Jalapeño Lime Vinaigrette

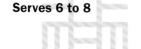

Serves 6 to 8

This recipe is a shout-out to summer, peak-season corn, and to chef Pierre Thiam, who has worked to bring an ancient African grain, fonio, to the masses. Here fonio's nutty flavor plays with grilled corn and a bright jalapeño lime vinaigrette, plus veggies, to create an array of colors and textures. Corn is naturally sweet, and once grilled, the lightly charred kernels pick up a delicious smoky note. The fonio in the recipe is fluffy and filling, while the vinaigrette delivers a hint-o-heat with sweet and tangy notes that make this salad all the more craveable. It's delicious as a salad dressing but also lovely drizzled over grain bowls, roasted meats, and grilled fish, chicken, and vegetables. It can easily be doubled and used as a marinade for fish and vegetables too, or whatever you grill to serve as a summertime main, with this salad on the side.

Vinaigrette

¼ cup fresh lime juice

½ small jalapeño pepper, stemmed and coarsely chopped

1 teaspoon ginger garlic puree, homemade (page 35) or store-bought

1 teaspoon kosher salt, plus more as needed

½ teaspoon honey

½ teaspoon sugar

½ cup avocado oil

2 tablespoons mayonnaise

1 tablespoon All-Day Seasoning Blend (page 35)

Zest and juice of 1 lime

Kosher salt

2 ears of corn, husks removed

¾ cup fonio (for sourcing, see page 26)

1 cup cherry tomatoes, halved

1 cup diced English cucumber

½ cup salted roasted cashews, coarsely chopped

¼ cup finely diced red onion

¼ cup (loosely packed) finely chopped fresh flat-leaf parsley leaves and tender stems

Freshly ground black pepper

Preheat a charcoal outdoor grill to high heat.

Make the vinaigrette: In a blender, combine the lime juice, jalapeño, ginger garlic puree, salt, honey, and sugar and blend until smooth. With the blender running, slowly drizzle in the oil until emulsified. Taste and adjust the seasoning. Set aside. (The vinaigrette will keep in an airtight container in the refrigerator for up to 1 week.)

In a small bowl, mix together the mayonnaise, seasoning blend, about half the lime zest, and the lime juice. Season with salt to taste. With a brush or your hands, slather the mayo mixture over the corn. Grill the corn, turning regularly, until charred and caramelized all over, 10 to 15 minutes total. (Alternatively, grill the corn on a stovetop grill pan or in a large cast-iron skillet over medium-high heat until charred all over, about 8 minutes.) Allow to cool slightly, then slice off the kernels: Flip a small bowl upside down and, placing the corn lengthwise on the base of the bowl, cut downward and away from you. Transfer the kernels to a small bowl.

In a small pot, combine the fonio and 2 cups of water. Cover and bring to a boil over medium-high heat. Reduce the heat to low and cook for 1 minute, then turn off the heat. Keep covered for 4 more minutes, then remove the lid and fluff with a fork. Set aside to cool.

Prepare the other salad ingredients: In a medium bowl, combine the cherry tomatoes, cucumber, cashews, onion, parsley, and remaining lime zest. Add the cooled fonio and grilled corn to the bowl. Season to taste with salt and pepper, then toss to combine. Toss with the vinaigrette and serve.

PICKLED OKRA AND CUCUMBER
with Yogurt Sauce

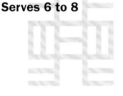

Serves 6 to 8

Okra and cucumbers are widely consumed vegetables in West Africa. Okra is often used in stews and soups and is most known for its thickening properties. Cucumbers are used more for their refreshing quality and are seen in salads and sandwiches. It wasn't until I spent some time in Kentucky, where pickled vegetables are common, that I saw these two veggies together in a way I had never experienced before. Before starting my season of *Top Chef,* I visited Kentucky on a recon mission to eat my way through the state and gain some knowledge of the local cuisine. At one stop, I enjoyed a deliciously tangy and cleansing plate of pickled okra and cucumber and thought, "Why haven't I had anything like this in Ghana?" Pickling is a technique that preserves food in a concentrated brine and is an excellent way to enjoy vegetables, especially when they are not in season. Traditionally, drying, smoking, and salting have been the go-to preservation techniques used in West Africa. But now, when I visit Ghana and West Africa, I get excited to see chefs like Fatmata Binta and Michael Adé Elégbèdé experimenting with pickling and fermenting indigenous African ingredients such as okra, currants, and star fruit.

Pickled Okra

12 ounces small to medium okra pods

6 sprigs of dill

2 garlic cloves

1 or 2 small dried piri piri chilies (for sourcing, see page 31) or Thai chilies, halved

½ tablespoon coriander seeds

1 teaspoon yellow mustard seeds

½ teaspoon celery seeds

½ teaspoon whole black peppercorns

½ teaspoon fennel seeds

1½ cups cane vinegar or apple cider vinegar

1½ cups filtered water, plus more as needed

2 tablespoons kosher salt

2 tablespoons sugar

Boiling water, as needed

Pickled Cucumbers

1 large English cucumber

1 teaspoon plus 1 tablespoon kosher salt

¾ cup cane vinegar or apple cider vinegar

¾ cup filtered water

2 tablespoons sugar

1 teaspoon whole black peppercorns

3 garlic cloves

Yogurt Sauce

2 cups plain whole milk yogurt

1 cup sour cream

2 tablespoons Roasted Garlic Puree (page 36)

¾ teaspoon kosher salt

½ teaspoon crushed red pepper flakes (optional)

To Serve

1 tablespoon high-quality extra-virgin olive oil

½ teaspoon crushed red pepper flakes

Lavash, bread, or crackers (optional)

Special Equipment

2 (16-ounce) wide-mouth canning jars with lids

1 (32-ounce) wide-mouth canning jar or 2 more 16-ounce wide-mouth jars with lids

Preheat the oven to 250°F.

Sterilize the jars (see Notes, page 128). Place the jars and lids in a large pot and cover with water until submerged. Bring to a simmer over medium-high heat and let simmer for 10 minutes. Keep the jars in the water until ready to fill. One at a time, carefully remove the jars with tongs, pouring out the water from the interior, and place them on a clean, heat-resistant surface.

Recipe continues

Make the pickled okra: Wash the okra thoroughly and trim off the stems. Slice the okra lengthwise into quarters. Between 2 sterilized 16-ounce canning jars, divide and pack the okra, dill, garlic, and chilies, standing the okra up vertically and alternating stems up and down.

In a medium saucepan over medium heat, toast the coriander seeds, mustard seeds, celery seeds, peppercorns, and fennel seeds, swirling the pan often to toast evenly, until fragrant, about 3 minutes. Add the vinegar, filtered water, salt, and sugar and bring to a boil over medium-high heat, stirring to dissolve the salt and sugar. Pour the mixture over the okra in the jars, leaving ½ inch of space between the top of the liquid and the lid. If there is not enough pickling liquid, add more filtered water. Release any air bubbles that might be trapped in the okra by running a clean thin-bladed knife around the inside of the jars, then seal the jars.

Place a metal trivet at the bottom of a large stockpot and fill the pot halfway with water. Bring the water to a boil and add the jars. Pour in more boiling water to cover the jars by at least 1 inch. Bring to a rolling boil, cover, and let simmer for 10 minutes. Turn off the heat, remove the lid, and let the jars stand in the water for 5 minutes. Using canning jar tongs, transfer the jars to a rack or towel to cool. Do not tilt, turn, or dry the jars, and do not disturb the lids or tighten the bands. Properly sealed jars will keep in a cool, dark place for up to 6 months. Refrigerate after opening.

(Alternatively, make a quick pickle. After pouring the boiling pickling liquid into the jars, immediately seal the jars and transfer them to the refrigerator. Okra will be ready in 1 week and will keep for 2 weeks.)

Make the pickled cucumbers: Slice the cucumber crosswise into ⅛-inch-thick coins and place in a colander. Toss the cucumbers with 1 teaspoon of the salt and mix well. Allow to sit and leach water for 10 minutes. Pat dry with paper towels, then place in the sterilized 32-ounce jar (or divide between two 16-ounce jars).

In a medium saucepan over medium-high heat, combine the vinegar, filtered water, sugar, peppercorns, garlic, and remaining 1 tablespoon of salt. Bring to a boil, stirring to dissolve the sugar and salt. Pour the mixture over the cucumbers in the jar. Seal the lid. Let cool at room temperature for 30 minutes. Refrigerate for 24 hours The pickles will keep in an airtight container in the refrigerator for up to 10 days.

Make the yogurt sauce: In a small bowl, mix the yogurt, sour cream, roasted garlic puree, salt, and pepper flakes (if using) until smooth and well combined.

To serve, smear the yogurt sauce on a platter. Remove a few large spoonfuls of okra and cucumbers from the pickling liquid and place on the yogurt. Drizzle with olive oil and sprinkle with red pepper flakes. Serve with lavash, bread, or crackers, or enjoy as is.

Notes: You can buy some components, like the yogurt sauce or pickles, if you don't have time to make all of them.

You can sterilize the canning jars either in boiling water as directed above or in a 250°F oven for 20 minutes. Then fill, boil, cool, and refrigerate as directed.

ROASTED CABBAGE
with Coconut Beurre Blanc

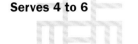

Serves 4 to 6

Both cabbage and coconut grow best in moist, warm climates, which is why they are two of the biggest agricultural exports Ghana has to offer. Green cabbage, the round, hardy, and subtly sweet variety, is the primary type exported and the focus for this dish. The cabbage is cut into thick wedges that develop sweet, nutty, and caramelized flavors when roasted. It's combined with a coconut beurre blanc, a French-inspired sauce that is rich and complex with the flavors of shallot, ginger, and coconut two ways: vinegar and cream. Serve them together as a vegetarian side dish, or as a main course with rice, and showcase two of Ghana's most humble ingredients in a modern way.

Cabbage

¼ cup high-quality extra-virgin olive oil

3 garlic cloves, finely chopped

1 teaspoon fresh thyme leaves

1 (2-pound) head of green cabbage, halved and cut into 1-inch-thick wedges

Kosher salt and freshly ground black pepper

Coconut Beurre Blanc

¼ cup dry white wine

¼ cup coconut vinegar or champagne vinegar

1 small shallot, finely chopped

1 (1-inch) piece of fresh ginger, peeled and finely chopped

⅓ cup coconut cream

¼ teaspoon kosher salt, plus more to taste

Freshly ground white pepper

1 cup (2 sticks) cold unsalted butter, cut into 1-tablespoon pieces

¼ cup store-bought crispy garlic, for garnish

Make the cabbage: Preheat the oven to 425°F.

In a small bowl, stir together the oil, garlic, and thyme. Arrange the cabbage wedges on a baking sheet, brush both sides with the garlic mixture, and season with salt and pepper.

Roast until fragrant and starting to char on the bottom, about 15 minutes. Flip the cabbage and roast until it is tender and the other side is starting to char, 10 to 15 minutes more. Remove the baking sheet from the oven and let cool slightly.

While the cabbage roasts, make the coconut beurre blanc: In a medium heavy-bottomed saucepan over medium heat, combine the wine, vinegar, shallot, and ginger. Bring to a boil and cook until syrupy and reduced to 2 to 3 tablespoons, about 5 minutes. Add the coconut cream, salt, and a pinch of white pepper and cook, whisking frequently, until well combined, about 1 minute. Reduce the heat to medium-low and whisk in 3 tablespoons of the butter until completely blended into the sauce. Whisking constantly, add the remaining butter 3 tablespoons at a time, adding more before the previous pieces have completely melted (the sauce should maintain the consistency of hollandaise). Remove the pan from the heat occasionally to prevent the sauce from breaking. Season to taste with more salt and white pepper. Pour the sauce through a fine-mesh sieve into a small heatproof bowl, pressing on and then discarding the solids.

Transfer the cabbage to a serving plate. Drizzle the sauce over the cabbage and sprinkle with some of the crispy garlic. Serve right away and be sure to pass around the remaining crispy garlic at the table.

ARUGULA SALAD
with Egusi Granola, Sorghum, and Sherry Vinaigrette

Serves 2 to 4

This is my go-to salad for any dinner party, not only because it's refreshing, but also because it utilizes an important ingredient. Sorghum is a cereal grain that is crucial to food security in Ghana because it's a versatile crop that can withstand different climates and harsh weather conditions, like drought or a dry season. Primarily grown in the northern region, sorghum is used to make porridge, fermented drinks, popular dishes like waakye, and so much more. Sweet sorghum syrup, made from the juice of the sorghum plant, is a thick, dark syrup that is similar in taste to molasses and is the base for the vinaigrette used in this salad. Goat cheese, pickled onions, and egusi granola add creamy, sharp, and nutty flavors.

Pickled Red Onion

½ cup (packed) julienned red onion

1 tablespoon coriander seeds

½ cup red wine vinegar

¼ cup sugar

2 tablespoons kosher salt

Vinaigrette

2 tablespoons sherry vinegar

1½ tablespoons sorghum syrup or maple syrup

1 tablespoon fresh lemon juice

¼ cup high-quality extra-virgin olive oil

Kosher salt and freshly ground black pepper

4 cups (packed) baby arugula

½ cup Egusi and Coconut Granola (page 57)

¼ cup crumbled goat cheese, or more to taste

Make the pickled red onion: In a large (at least 2-cup) heatproof jar or another nonreactive lidded container, combine the onion and coriander seeds.

In a medium pot over medium-high heat, combine the red wine vinegar, sugar, and salt with ⅓ cup of water. Bring to a simmer, stirring to dissolve the sugar and salt, then pour the hot liquid over the onion. Seal with the lid and cool to room temperature, about 30 minutes, then use immediately or refrigerate for up to 2 weeks.

Make the vinaigrette: In a small bowl, whisk together the sherry vinegar, sorghum syrup, and lemon juice. Continue whisking and slowly drizzle in the olive oil until everything is incorporated and smooth. Season with salt and pepper to taste. The vinaigrette will keep in an airtight container in the refrigerator for up to 1 week.

In a large serving bowl, combine the arugula with ¼ cup of the vinaigrette, or enough vinaigrette to lightly coat the greens. Add the granola and goat cheese. Drain the pickled onion and add to the salad. Toss if you like, and serve immediately.

PAW PAW SALAD
Papaya Salad

Serves 2 to 4

Agriculture is the most significant sector of Ghana's economy. Papaya, also known as paw paw (not to be confused with the fruit found in the eastern United States by the same name), is a massively important crop in Ghana because it can be grown pretty much anywhere. In Ghana, both ripe and unripe papaya are eaten fresh, in smoothies and in salads. It's an ingredient that becomes more complex as it ripens. This dish uses crunchy, green, unripe papaya. It's a play off a Thai-style salad that highlights clean-tasting, crispy paw paw and the crunch of peanuts with a bit of heat and acidity. If you can't find paw paw, use daikon radish or jicama.

Kosher salt

10 green beans, ends trimmed and halved lengthwise

1 cup julienned green papaya (see Note)

10 cherry tomatoes, halved

5 or 6 scallions, thinly sliced (white and green parts)

¼ cup (packed) fresh cilantro leaves, plus more for garnish

½ cup Paw Paw Dressing (recipe follows), or to taste

2 tablespoons coarsely chopped salted roasted peanuts, for garnish

Fill a medium saucepan with water, bring to a boil, and lightly salt the water. Cook the green beans until crisp-tender, about 1 minute. Drain and rinse under cold water, then cut in half lengthwise. Place the green beans in a medium bowl, then add the papaya, tomatoes, scallions, and cilantro. Gradually add the dressing and toss to combine well. Taste and add more dressing if desired. Sprinkle with the peanuts and garnish with cilantro leaves. Serve immediately.

Note: To prepare the papaya, peel the fruit, cut it in half, and remove the seeds. Use a julienne peeler to cut the flesh.

Paw Paw Dressing
Makes about 2 cups

This tart and spicy dressing is great on salads or grilled veggies. It has a funky backbone thanks to a hit of fish sauce.

¾ cup sugar

½ cup plus 2 tablespoons fresh lime juice

¼ cup plus 2 tablespoons smashed garlic cloves

¼ cup plus 2 tablespoons hot water

¼ cup plus 1 tablespoon cane vinegar

¼ cup fish sauce

2 teaspoons Mom's Hot Pepper Sauce (page 43), or store-bought Scotch bonnet hot sauce

In a blender, puree the sugar, lime juice, garlic, hot water, cane vinegar, fish sauce, and hot pepper sauce until smooth. The dressing will keep in an airtight container in the refrigerator for up to 10 days.

TOMATO ON TOMATO

Serves 6 to 8

As you'll notice throughout this book and a lot of West African cuisine, tomatoes (in all forms) are extremely popular. When I was younger, I hated raw tomatoes with a fiery passion. The fruit didn't appeal to me unless it was stewed or in ketchup form. It wasn't until I was in college, at Johnson & Wales University in Providence, Rhode Island, that my opinion drastically changed. I interned and eventually worked at a restaurant called Nicks on Broadway, where we served a local summer tomato dish with pickled elements. Initially, I was very skeptical, but when I tasted it, it blew me away with the brightness and textures that the tomatoes took on in the dish. This recipe is inspired by that experience and showcases tomatoes, an important West African ingredient, in a way that blends West African and New American techniques. It celebrates all that's great about the humble tomato. Tangy, robust, umami, and savory are all of the flavor notes you'll pick up, plus a ton of crunch from the breadcrumb topping. My favorite time to make this dish is either when I'm in Ghana or when I'm stateside during the summer months, when tomatoes are most flavorful and juicy.

Pickled Tomatoes

- 1½ pounds heirloom tomatoes (2 or 3 large tomatoes)
- 1 cup (packed) coarsely chopped fresh flat-leaf parsley leaves and tender stems
- ½ cup (packed) coarsely chopped fresh basil leaves
- 1 large shallot, minced
- 2 tablespoons fresh lime juice
- 2 tablespoons champagne vinegar
- 1 tablespoon (packed) light brown sugar
- 2 teaspoons kosher salt
- 2 teaspoons Mom's Hot Pepper Sauce (page 43), or store-bought Scotch bonnet hot sauce
- 1 teaspoon cumin seeds, ground

Seasoned Breadcrumbs

- 2 tablespoons unsalted butter
- ¾ cup panko breadcrumbs
- 3 tablespoons (loosely packed) finely chopped fresh flat-leaf parsley leaves
- 1 tablespoon (loosely packed) finely chopped fresh thyme leaves
- 2 teaspoons freshly grated lime zest
- Kosher salt

Roasted Tomato Sauce

- 3 Roma tomatoes, quartered
- 4 tablespoons high-quality extra-virgin olive oil
- 2 teaspoons kosher salt, plus more to taste
- 2 medium yellow onions, thinly sliced
- 1½ cups whole milk
- ½ cup heavy cream
- 1 tablespoon All-Day Seasoning Blend (page 35)
- Toasted bread or cooked white rice, for serving

Make the pickled tomatoes: Slice the heirloom tomatoes into ¼-inch-thick rounds. In a medium nonreactive container or bowl, whisk together the parsley, basil, shallot, lime juice, vinegar, sugar, salt, hot pepper sauce, and cumin until well combined. Add the tomatoes, cover, and transfer to the refrigerator to marinate for 4 to 8 hours.

While the tomatoes marinate, make the seasoned breadcrumbs: In a medium skillet over medium heat, melt the butter until it starts to foam, then add the panko. Cook, stirring often, until the butter smells nutty and the panko is deeply golden,

Recipe continues

134 *Ghana to the World*

3 to 5 minutes, then transfer to a bowl to cool. When cool, stir in the parsley, thyme, and lime zest and season with salt to taste.

Make the roasted tomato sauce: Preheat the oven to 450°F. Line a rimmed baking sheet with parchment paper.

Place the Roma tomatoes on the prepared baking sheet and toss with 2 tablespoons of the olive oil and the salt. Roast until the tomatoes take on a little color and soften up, 20 to 25 minutes.

Meanwhile, heat the remaining 2 tablespoons of olive oil in a large heavy-bottomed saucepan over medium-low heat. When the oil is hot, add the onions and cook, stirring often, until completely soft, 20 to 25 minutes. Add the milk, cream, roasted tomatoes, and seasoning blend, stirring to combine. Bring to a simmer and cook, stirring every 10 minutes or so, until most of the liquid has evaporated, about 1 hour.

Allow the sauce to cool slightly, then transfer to a blender and puree until smooth. Pass through a fine-mesh sieve into a medium bowl, then season with salt to taste.

To serve, spread roasted tomato sauce on the bottom of a serving plate. Using a slotted spoon, scoop the pickled tomatoes from the brine and arrange them on top of the sauce. Top with the seasoned breadcrumbs and serve with toasted bread or white rice.

GLAZED CARROTS
with Benne Seeds

Serves 4

Glazed carrots are a classic culinary school dish that professors use to teach boiling, glazing, and sauce-making techniques to new cooks. This recipe comes from those days at culinary school. It's my take using whole carrots and carrot juice to reinforce that carrot flavor, and with a good punch of ginger, garlic, cumin, and paprika. You can typically find fresh carrot juice in your grocery store's produce section.

1 pound small carrots, tops trimmed, peeled and left whole or halved lengthwise if more than ½ inch thick

3 tablespoons ginger garlic puree, homemade (page 35) or store-bought

2 tablespoons neutral oil

1 tablespoon ground cumin

½ tablespoon smoked paprika

1 tablespoon kosher salt, plus more as needed

5 sprigs of thyme

Glaze

2 cups fresh carrot juice

1 cup fresh orange juice

1 cup white wine vinegar

¼ cup soy sauce

1 cup ketchup

½ cup amber honey

1 (½-inch) piece of fresh ginger, peeled and minced

1 cup (packed) fresh cilantro leaves

½ cup (1 stick) cold unsalted butter, diced

Zest and juice of 1 lime, plus more juice as needed

2 teaspoons benne seeds (for sourcing, see page 25) or sesame seeds, for garnish

½ small bunch chives, thinly sliced, for garnish

Preheat the oven to 400°F.

In a large bowl, season the carrots with the ginger garlic puree, oil, cumin, paprika, and salt. Toss to coat. Arrange the carrots on a rimmed baking sheet large enough to accommodate them all in a single layer, spread the thyme sprigs over the carrots, and cover tightly with foil. Roast until the carrots are slightly softened, about 20 minutes.

While the carrots roast, make the glaze: In a wide, medium sauté pan over high heat, combine the carrot juice, orange juice, vinegar, and soy sauce. Bring to a boil and cook, stirring occasionally, until reduced by half, about 10 minutes. Reduce the heat so the mixture simmers, then whisk in the ketchup, honey, and ginger. Add half the cilantro to steep, and continue cooking for 5 minutes. Remove the cilantro and squeeze any liquid back into the pan. Reduce the heat to low, then immediately add the butter a few pieces at a time, stirring constantly and waiting until the previous batch of butter is emulsified before adding the next. Add the lime zest and juice and a pinch of salt, then taste and add more lime juice if necessary. Set aside (you should have about 2½ cups of glaze).

Remove the foil and baste the carrots with a little less than half of the glaze. Return the carrots to the oven, uncovered, and roast, turning the carrots halfway through cooking, until they are tender in the middle and brown and caramelized at the edges, an additional 20 to 25 minutes. Remove the thyme, then brush the carrots with a little more glaze.

Transfer the carrots to a serving plate, garnish with the benne seeds, chives, and remaining cilantro, and serve immediately. Leftover glaze will keep in an airtight container in the refrigerator for up to 7 days.

COLLARD GREENS
with Coconut Milk

Serves 5 to 6

Who doesn't love a big, hot bowl of perfectly cooked collard greens? In my travels I've noticed that each place Africans have touched has its own version of stewed greens: in the Caribbean, callaloo greens are stewed until tender; in the American South, collard greens with neck bones are common; and in Brazil, collards are stewed with smoky bacon. This dish combines those influences into a savory yet slightly sweet side dish.

2 pounds collard greens

2 tablespoons virgin coconut oil

1 medium yellow onion, minced

2 tablespoons peeled and grated fresh ginger

2 garlic cloves, minced

1 (2-pound) fully cooked smoked turkey drumstick or 2 pounds smoked turkey wings and/or neck

1 cup reduced-sodium chicken stock

1 cup full-fat coconut milk

¼ cup sherry vinegar

1 teaspoon crushed red pepper flakes

½ teaspoon kosher salt

Remove the stem from each collard leaf. Working in batches as necessary, wash the collards several times in cold water to remove any dirt. Pat dry between kitchen towels, then stack a few leaves at a time, roll up like a cigar, and cut crosswise into ¼-inch-thick ribbons.

In a large Dutch oven, heat the coconut oil over medium heat. When it shimmers, add the onion and cook, stirring often, until it just starts to take on a golden color, 5 to 7 minutes. Add the ginger and garlic and cook, stirring, until fragrant, about 1 minute. Add the turkey drumstick, stock, coconut milk, ½ cup of water, the vinegar, red pepper flakes, and salt and stir to combine.

Bring to a simmer and cook, uncovered, until reduced by about one-third, about 15 minutes. Add the collards and continue to cook, stirring occasionally, until the greens are tender, about 15 minutes. Remove from the heat and, if desired, remove the turkey meat completely, or shred the meat and add it back into the collards. Serve immediately.

STARCHES, RICE, AND SWALLOWS

Learning to Tell My Story

I think for any artist early in the process of learning a craft, the impulse is to look to experts in your field for inspiration, to learn how to do, or how to express. In culinary school and in my career afterward, I looked to other chefs and cuisines as the pinnacle of my profession. I learned French technique and worked at an Italian restaurant, learning how to manipulate certain ingredients to make dishes that spoke to those cultures. It wasn't until I worked at Nuela, a Peruvian restaurant, that I saw the culture I had grown up in. There, I worked with chef Erik Ramirez (who now runs Llama Inn and Llama San in New York) and found a lot of joy working in the back of the house. It made sense to me: building flavors through peppers, ginger, and chilies reminded me of West African sauces and techniques.

Chef Ramirez was the first person to call me "chef," which instilled my confidence in myself. The way in which Nuela served and promoted Peruvian food, drinks, and culture showed me that you can tell your story in an uncompromising way. You can make food that not only is delicious and captivating but also tells stories, with feeling and emotion that come from having a connection to the culture behind it.

When you are finally comfortable enough in your craft, you begin looking inward, trusting that the things you've learned can help you tell your own story instead of merely repeating what others have done.

While I was still a line cook, I started thinking about telling my own story and making food that reflected my life. I was yearning for depth and connection to the things I was cooking. I wanted it to say something, anything, about the life that I knew and had lived. One of the biggest blessings of my life, both then and now, is that I've been able to see and tap into cooking knowledge on both sides of the Atlantic. I can call upon ancient ingredients and practices of West Africa, some that I'm still learning, and I can also connect with chefs here who call upon generations and generations of Black cooking in America. It's wonderful because it gives me so much to explore and share.

Climbing the metaphorical tree ("Woforo Dua Pa a," see page 118) also allowed me to see the ways in which I could combine my own culinary foundation with the things I was learning. I knew I wanted to tell stories with my food using West African flavors and ingredients but mixed together in my own way. There's such a large knowledge pool of ingredients, techniques, and dishes in West African cuisines that I knew I could tap into, but I wanted to combine them with new flavors and presentations I experienced in culinary school or from working in Italian and French restaurants. A traditional dish like fufu with light soup, groundnut soup, or palm nut soup could be served in an avant-garde way. Frying the fufu and pouring the soup tableside creates a different presentation but is still true to the original dish and flavors that go back hundreds of years. African food is minimized in global food culture, but it's just as elegant, complex, and varied as any other cuisine.

It's important to me as a chef to still be locked into honoring the original dishes while creating an updated way to experience this food. That can be such a beautiful, powerful experience when people with African heritage see themselves reflected in fine dining. That's not to say the way African food is traditionally served isn't also a beautiful presentation, but there's variety in African dining experiences, and we should embrace that.

Even today with all of the accolades and attention that Black chefs across the diaspora are receiving for their work, it still feels like traditional West African cooking isn't given the respect it deserves. African cooking is seen and described as humble—as if it can't be complex and nuanced—and is framed as foreign despite being the basis of so many dishes around the world. There's an entire breadth of regional African cuisine, techniques, specialties, and ingredients that have yet to be fully explored by media and diners, in the same way regional Italian or Thai cooking and recipes have been in recent years. The food world still has a bit of climbing to do as well.

In this way I think that a lot of Black chefs like myself are protectors and guides of West African cuisine and Black cooking in this country. We're building on a vast number of techniques and ingredients and bringing it to the present moment. We're also making connections to other parts of the world that we've noticed either through traveling or researching other cuisines, all while we get better at our craft. And those lessons can come from looking at the work of home cooks as well as professional chefs. Cooking is a career and a job, but it also requires committing yourself to being part of a bigger story that will move forward. We belong to a lineage, tradition, and culture, and we bring that into the fold when we cook. That's a lot to put on ourselves, but it also feels like the duty and lesson of sankofa when you make a name for yourself.

Looking back, my time as a line cook really served a greater purpose because it helped me hone my craft. It also taught me how to be methodical in my work and have emotional intelligence in my interactions with those around me. I had to learn to meet people where they were at and get to know where they were coming from.

Experience is a great thing because it provides a foundation for when your skills can finally meet the vision that you have for yourself. The moment when I finally felt like I could use my skills to tell the exact story I wanted to tell was so beautiful. It's the moment that makes you feel like you've become elite at your craft, but you can't rest there. Continuing to push yourself to improve is what separates the good from the great. Excellence is the constant pursuit of creativity, skill, and craftsmanship. It's a lifelong, unending process of learning and exposing yourself to new things, but it's worth it.

SILKY YAM PUREE

Serves 8 to 10

Believe it or not, sweet potatoes and yams are two totally different tubers, but they're both important ingredients in the American South that I love cooking with. Yams are native to Africa and Asia and tend to be bigger than sweet potatoes, which are native to the Americas. If you're looking for a luscious side dish with a touch of natural sweetness that's easy to prepare, this is a great option. It's a wonderful complement for a composed dish like Sticky Tamarind-Glazed Duck Legs (page 218), or even Shito Fried Chicken (page 215). The texture is silky smooth, and there's plenty of room to get creative with your flavors by adding savory ingredients such as Parmesan cheese, spices like allspice, or different sweeteners like maple syrup.

3 pounds yam (about 1 large)

1 tablespoon kosher salt, plus more to taste

⅓ cup whole milk

2 tablespoons (packed) light brown sugar or maple syrup

2 teaspoons ground nutmeg

½ teaspoon finely ground white pepper

½ cup (1 stick) unsalted butter, cut into 1-inch pieces

Peel the yam down to its bright orange flesh, removing any brown spots as best as possible. Cut it into ½-inch cubes and put them in a large pot in a single layer. Add water to cover by at least 1 inch and season with the salt. Bring to a boil over high heat, then reduce the heat to medium and cook until the yam cubes are very tender and almost falling apart, about 15 minutes. Drain and place the yam in a food processor.

Pour the milk in the pot you cooked the yam in and bring to a simmer over medium heat. Pour the milk into the food processor with the yam. Add the brown sugar, nutmeg, and white pepper. Puree until smooth, adding the butter a few pieces at a time and waiting until one batch is fully incorporated into the puree before adding the next.

Remove the puree from the food processor and season to taste with more salt. Serve immediately.

BAKED RED PEAS

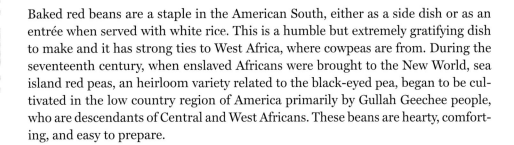

Serves 4 to 6

Baked red beans are a staple in the American South, either as a side dish or as an entrée when served with white rice. This is a humble but extremely gratifying dish to make and it has strong ties to West Africa, where cowpeas are from. During the seventeenth century, when enslaved Africans were brought to the New World, sea island red peas, an heirloom variety related to the black-eyed pea, began to be cultivated in the low country region of America primarily by Gullah Geechee people, who are descendants of Central and West Africans. These beans are hearty, comforting, and easy to prepare.

1 cup dried sea island red peas

2 tablespoons high-quality extra-virgin olive oil

1 (4-ounce) piece of smoked slab bacon, skin removed, cut into 1-inch chunks

1 medium yellow onion, finely diced

3 garlic cloves, minced

1 teaspoon kosher salt

1 (28-ounce) can whole peeled tomatoes

3 tablespoons All-Day Seasoning Blend (page 35)

10 sprigs of thyme

2 fresh bay leaves

¼ cup molasses or sorghum syrup

2 tablespoons cane vinegar

Rinse the peas, then put them in a large bowl and cover with a few inches of cool water. Soak, covered, at room temperature for 4 to 8 hours. Drain the peas.

Preheat the oven to 325°F.

In a medium Dutch oven or other ovenproof pot over high heat, heat the oil. When it shimmers, add the bacon and cook until it starts to render some fat and crisp up, about 2 minutes. Add the onion, garlic, and salt. Cook, stirring often, until the onion is translucent and the bacon is crisp, 3 minutes.

Gently crush the tomatoes in their can, then add them to the pot along with the drained peas, seasoning blend, thyme sprigs, bay leaves, molasses, and ¾ cup of water. Stir, bring to a simmer, and place the lid on the pot.

Transfer the pot to the oven and bake until the peas are completely tender without falling apart, about 1 hour. (Alternatively, simmer over medium-low heat on the stove for about 1 hour, or cook in a pressure cooker for 15 to 20 minutes.) Remove the thyme and bay leaves, stir in the vinegar, and serve.

RED RED STEW

Serves 6

In America, especially in the South, black-eyed peas are best known as a good luck and prosperity meal on New Year's Day. In Africa, this awesome source of protein, eaten year-round, is used in all forms: ground, dried, fresh, and in stews like red red. I bet if you were to sample a group of Ghanaians about their favorite local dishes, red red would automatically be in the top five they list off. It's a hearty vegetarian stew that traditionally contains ripe red tomatoes and red palm oil—which is where the dish gets its name—plus onions and spices. This recipe is a traditional take on the iconic dish. It's savory because of the peas and the palm oil, and a little sweet because of the plantains. You can make your red red soupier or heartier by either leaving the cooked beans as is or crushing half of them for more body, depending on what you prefer. Red red can also be served with gari, a coarse cassava meal.

Black-Eyed Peas

3 cups dried black-eyed peas

1 garlic clove, crushed

2 sprigs of rosemary

1 tablespoon kosher salt

½ teaspoon baking soda

Red Red

2 tablespoons virgin coconut oil

4 tablespoons red palm oil (see Notes, page 98)

1 large red onion, finely diced

1 (1-inch) piece of fresh ginger, finely grated

3 garlic cloves, finely grated

½ red Scotch bonnet pepper, finely chopped

1 (14.5-ounce) can crushed tomatoes

4 medium Roma tomatoes, coarsely chopped

2 tablespoons crayfish powder (optional; for sourcing, see page 25)

1 tablespoon tomato paste

1 teaspoon chili powder

2 teaspoons kosher salt, plus more to taste

1 teaspoon freshly ground black pepper

Fried Plantains

2 ripe plantains (yellow with some black or brown spots)

¼ teaspoon kosher salt

½ cup neutral oil

Sliced avocado, for serving

Gari, for serving (for sourcing, see page 26)

Make the black-eyed peas: In a medium bowl, cover the black-eyed peas with a few inches of cool water and soak, covered, at room temperature for 4 to 8 hours.

Rinse and drain the black-eyed peas and place in a large pot with 8 cups of water, the garlic, rosemary, and salt. Bring to a boil, then reduce the heat and simmer for 30 minutes. Add the baking soda and continue to cook until the beans are soft enough to crush between your fingers, about 15 minutes. Remove the garlic and rosemary, then drain the beans and set aside.

Make the red red: In a large pot over medium-high heat, heat the coconut oil and 2 tablespoons of the palm oil until it shimmers. Add the onion and cook, stirring frequently, until translucent, 8 to 10 minutes. Add the ginger, garlic, and Scotch bonnet and cook for 3 more minutes. Reduce the heat to medium, then add the crushed and Roma tomatoes, crayfish powder (if using), tomato paste, chili powder, salt, and black pepper. Cook, stirring frequently, until the oil starts to rise to the surface, about 20 minutes. Add the drained beans to the pot. Stir the sauce and beans together and cook over low heat for 10 minutes, then add the remaining 2 tablespoons of palm oil. Season with more salt to taste if desired. Keep warm.

Recipe continues

Make the fried plantains: Line a plate with paper towels. Peel the plantains by slicing about ½ inch off the ends. Carefully score just the skin down the middle and peel it off. Slice the plantains at an angle into ½-inch-thick pieces. Lay the plantain pieces on a plate and sprinkle with the salt. Pour the neutral oil into a large frying pan and set over medium-low heat. Heat the oil until shimmering, then carefully add the plantains to the hot oil and cook until golden brown, about 7 minutes on each side. Transfer the plantains to the paper towels to drain before serving.

Serve the red red topped with fried plantains, sliced avocado, and gari. The stew will keep in an airtight container in the refrigerator for 7 days.

COCONUT RICE

Serves 4

Coconut rice is a common sight in many homes of African descendants. Africans brought their knowledge of coconut farming and cooking techniques to parts of the Americas, including the Caribbean and Brazil. Now coconut rice is a staple in Afro-Caribbean and Afro-Latin cuisines and is such an amazing side for meals like Coconut Curry Chickpeas with Mustard Greens (page 152) and Roasted Cabbage with Coconut Beurre Blanc (page 129) because of the slight sweetness the coconut milk brings.

1½ cups jasmine or basmati rice

1 (13.5-ounce) can full-fat coconut milk

1 teaspoon sugar

Kosher salt

Thoroughly rinse the rice in a fine-mesh sieve under running water until the water runs clear (see Note).

In a medium saucepan, combine the coconut milk, 1 cup of water, the sugar, and a pinch of salt. Stir until the sugar is dissolved. Stir in the rice. Bring to a boil over medium heat, then cover, reduce the heat to low, and cook until the rice is tender and the liquid is absorbed, 18 to 20 minutes. Remove from the heat and allow to rest, covered, for 10 minutes before fluffing with a fork and serving right away.

Note: Many of the recipes in this chapter focus on rice, one of my favorite things to eat. You'll notice most of them call for the rice to be rinsed. This isn't super complicated: Take a bowl of cool or lukewarm water and add your rice to it. Run your fingers through the rice and then carefully tip the bowl into the sink, using your hand to hold back the rice while you drain the water into the sink. I usually repeat the process 2 or 3 more times. Alternatively, you can put the rice in a fine-mesh sieve and rinse it under cool or lukewarm running water. We are looking to remove as much starch from the rice as possible so the grains remain separate.

COCONUT CURRY CHICKPEAS
with Mustard Greens

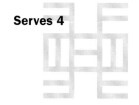

Serves 4

This recipe, like the Sweet Potato Peanut Stew (page 105), came off the On The Double menu I was planning before the pandemic. I was able to pivot, and I've now taught this dish countless times via online classes. It was by far my most popular recipe because of how easy it is to assemble and how flavorful the final product is. I found that chickpeas work really well in this dish because they can be stewed down to a beautiful soft texture that still holds its integrity as it cooks. Make it completely vegan by using vegetable stock or water instead of chicken stock. This dish is very simple in preparation but complex in flavor and an awesome intro to Caribbean flavors for those who've never experienced cuisine from this part of the world.

3 tablespoons neutral oil

1 medium yellow onion, finely diced

1 red bell pepper, stemmed, seeded, and finely diced

5 scallions, thinly sliced (white and green parts), plus more for garnish if desired

3 tablespoons fresh thyme leaves

3 tablespoons curry powder, homemade (page 39) or store-bought

5 garlic cloves, thinly sliced

2 teaspoons Mom's Hot Pepper Sauce (page 43) or store-bought Scotch bonnet hot sauce

2 tablespoons tomato paste

2 cups reduced-sodium chicken stock, vegetable stock, or water

1 (13.5-ounce) can full-fat coconut milk

2 teaspoons kosher salt, plus more to taste

2 (15-ounce) cans organic chickpeas, rinsed and drained

2 cups (packed) mustard greens, stemmed and coarsely chopped

Juice of 1 lemon

Coconut Rice (page 151), for serving

In a large pot over medium-high heat, heat the oil until it shimmers. Add the onion and bell pepper and sauté, stirring, until the vegetables have softened, about 7 minutes. Add the scallions, thyme, curry powder, garlic, and hot pepper sauce and cook until fragrant, 1 to 2 minutes. Add the tomato paste and cook, stirring, until the mixture has darkened to a brick red, an additional 2 minutes.

Add the chicken stock and coconut milk, then season with the salt. Bring to a boil, then reduce the heat to medium-low. Add the chickpeas and let the mixture simmer until reduced by about one-third, 10 to 15 minutes. Fold in the mustard greens and cook until wilted, an additional 3 to 5 minutes. Add the lemon juice, then taste and adjust the seasoning with additional salt. Serve immediately over coconut rice, and garnished with more scallions if desired.

SWEET FRIED PLANTAINS
with Benne Miso, Benne Seeds, and Onions

Serves 4

I could probably eat my weight in plantains if allowed. They're sweet, starchy, easy to make, and absolutely delicious, especially when perfectly caramelized, like the fried plantains in this recipe. When shopping, look for the yellow, ripe—but not overly ripe—fruit. Their sweetness is balanced with a ton of umami, by way of the benne miso made by a company called Keepwell Vinegar. Miso is fermented soybean paste from Asia, but this version has the addition of the West African benne seed, and is a toastier, nuttier, more savory miso than you may be used to. If you're not able to use Keepwell's product, I suggest brown or red miso for a comparable flavor profile. I also want to give a shout-out to chefs Adam Schop and Erik Ramirez from my days of working at Nuela in New York City. At the time, I saw plantains only as a household ingredient, never celebrated in culinary school or when I was working in other kitchens. Adam and Erik really honored not-so-luxurious ingredients with their cooking in a way that I still admire. Their love for plantains is just as deep as mine.

- 3 large ripe yellow plantains (see Note)
- 4 tablespoons peanut oil, for frying
- 1 medium yellow onion, halved and sliced into ⅛-inch-thick half-moons
- 3 garlic cloves, halved
- 2 teaspoons (packed) light brown sugar
- 2 teaspoons benne miso (for sourcing, see page 25) or brown or red miso
- 1 tablespoon sherry vinegar
- ½ teaspoon kosher salt
- 1 tablespoon fresh thyme leaves
- 2 teaspoons benne seeds (for sourcing, see page 25) or sesame seeds, for garnish

Peel the plantains by trimming about ½ inch off each end. Cut a lengthwise slit just through the peel, then remove and discard it. Cut the fruit crosswise into ¾-inch-thick rounds.

Line a plate with paper towels. In a large, heavy frying pan or cast-iron skillet over medium heat, warm 2 tablespoons of the peanut oil until it shimmers. Add the plantains, flat sides down, in a single layer and cook until golden brown on the first side, about 4 minutes. Reduce the heat slightly, then flip to cook the second side until golden brown, 4 minutes more. Continue to cook the plantain pieces, turning to brown the rounded sides every minute or so, until they're browned all over and fully soft inside, about 3 minutes more. Test one plantain by slicing it open; the center should be warm and soft. Using tongs, transfer the plantains to the paper towels.

Add the remaining 2 tablespoons of peanut oil to the pan and warm over medium heat until it shimmers. Add the onion and cook, stirring occasionally, until light brown around the edges, 3 to 5 minutes. Reduce the heat to medium-low, add the garlic, and continue cooking, stirring occasionally, until the onion is tender and deep golden with brown edges, 10 minutes more. Add the brown sugar and miso and cook, stirring, until the sugar has gotten sticky, 2 more minutes, then deglaze with 3 tablespoons of water and the sherry vinegar and stir in the salt. Return the plantains to the pan, add the thyme, and cook, stirring occasionally, until the sauce is glossy, about 3 minutes.

Transfer to a platter, garnish with benne seeds, and serve immediately.

Note: Avoid overripe black plantains as they will absorb a lot of oil while frying.

KONTOMIRE ABOMU

Serves 6

At my grandparents' home in Kumasi I would run after vendors yelling, "Kotonbre! Kotonbre!" My deep love of the dish that I expressed as a toddler has become a running joke in my family about where my love of food started. It's another classic stew in Ghana and has long been a favorite of mine because there's a fermented funk with a salty back note thanks to salted tilapia (koobi). My favorite source for koobi is Opparrel, an online marketplace that offers koobi with a strong scent that delivers on amazing flavor.

Around the world you'll see the substitution of spinach in place of cocoyam leaves (the leaves that grow as part of the cocoyam, a starchy tuber found in Ghana) because spinach is easier to come by, so feel free to do that too if you can't find cocoyam in the frozen food section at your local African market. I like to serve this dish with boiled puna yam but you can also serve it with white rice or boiled starchy plantains (the green ones).

1 medium koobi (dried salted tilapia) or any dried white fish (about 1 pound)

2 unripe green plantains

2 large eggs

1 bunch kontomire (cocoyam/taro root leaves; or mature spinach), stemmed and cut into 1-inch ribbons or 2 cups (packed) frozen kontomire

1 medium Roma tomato

¼ cup turkey berries (preferably fresh but canned is okay)

1 medium red onion, half chopped, half sliced ¼ inch thick

1 Scotch bonnet pepper or habanero pepper

3 teaspoons kosher salt

2 teaspoons red palm oil (see Notes, page 98)

2 teaspoons virgin coconut oil

1 avocado, sliced, for serving

Boiled puna yam, for serving

In a medium bowl, cover the koobi with 1 inch of water. Cover with plastic wrap and soak in the refrigerator for at least 8 hours or overnight, to reduce the salt content. Drain off the water.

Using a sharp knife, cut ½ inch off the ends of each plantain. Score the plantain peel lengthwise, remove the peel, carefully use the knife to scrape any film off the fruit, and rinse under cool water. Cut each plantain in half lengthwise, then in half again crosswise.

Fill a large pot with water and place a fitted steamer over the top to cover, making sure the water doesn't touch the steamer, then bring to a boil over high heat. Fill a small bowl with ice water. Add the koobi, plantains, and eggs to the water in the pot, then add the cocoyam leaves to the steamer. Cook everything until tender, 10 to 15 minutes. (If the rest takes longer, remove the eggs after 10 minutes, shock in the ice water, and peel.) Transfer all of the ingredients to a plate and cover with a dish towel to keep them warm.

Over an open flame or in a cast-iron pan over high heat, blister the tomato and turkey berries, until the tomato and turkey berries are considerably wilted, 3 to 5 minutes. Remove from the pan and set aside.

Recipe continues

In an asanka or a large mortar and pestle, combine the chopped onion, Scotch bonnet, steamed cocoyam leaves, tomato, turkey berries, and 2 teaspoons of the salt. Blend until the mixture is uniform and takes on a green color. (A food processor can also be used to combine the ingredients; pulse for 3 seconds at a time until the mixture is a uniform consistency.)

In a medium sauté pan over medium-high heat, heat the palm oil and coconut oil until shimmering. Add the sliced onion and cook, stirring often, until tender, 5 to 8 minutes. Season with the remaining 1 teaspoon of salt. Set aside.

In a large communal bowl or asanka, pour in the blended cocoyam mixture, then arrange the plantains, koobi, and whole eggs on top. Add the cooked onion with some of the oils from the pan. Serve immediately with sliced avocado and boiled puna yam.

JOLLOF RICE

Serves 6 to 8

When home chefs who are unfamiliar with West African cuisine ask me about jollof rice, I tell them, "If aliens were to visit West Africa and ask for a meal to represent the culture, seven out of ten people would serve them jollof." This rice dish is an integral part of Ghanaian and West African cuisine and a must at every family event. Cooking it highlights one of the mother sauces of West African cooking: the red stew. Bold and slightly spicy, it's made from cooking a puree of raw ingredients until they meld together into a sauce that flavors each grain of rice. That red stew is the genesis of so many dishes in West Africa, like the Fante Fante Fish Stew (page 97) and Waakye Stew (page 95). Jollof is our cuisine's Indian curry or our matzo ball soup in that many families and grandmothers have their own recipe for it. This is my family's version. Take your time building the flavors in the red stew and watch and smell as it develops in flavor as it cooks.

2 cups jasmine rice (see Note, page 151)

1 large red or Spanish onion, coarsely chopped

2 Roma tomatoes, coarsely chopped

½ large red bell pepper, stemmed, seeded, and coarsely chopped

1 Scotch bonnet or habanero pepper

3 garlic cloves

1 (1-inch) piece of fresh ginger, peeled and sliced

1 teaspoon anise seeds

½ cup neutral oil

2 tablespoons virgin coconut oil

½ medium Spanish onion, thinly sliced

2 heaping tablespoons tomato paste

2 teaspoons curry powder, homemade (page 39) or store-bought

1 teaspoon smoked paprika

1 teaspoon ground nutmeg

1 Maggi seasoning cube (for sourcing, see page 31)

2 fresh bay leaves

1 tablespoon kosher salt, plus more to taste

1½ cups reduced-sodium chicken stock

Thoroughly rinse the rice in a fine-mesh sieve under running water until the water runs clear.

In a blender, process the red onion, tomatoes, bell pepper, Scotch bonnet, garlic, ginger, and anise seeds until smooth.

In a heavy-bottomed pot over medium-high heat, heat both the neutral and coconut oils. When the oil shimmers, add the sliced Spanish onion and cook, stirring often, until translucent, about 4 minutes. Add the tomato paste, curry powder, paprika, nutmeg, and Maggi seasoning cube and cook until the spices and bouillon are well incorporated, about 5 more minutes. Add the tomato mixture and bay leaves and cook down, whisking occasionally, until most of the liquid has evaporated, about 45 minutes. (You're looking to cook the raw flavors out.) Stir in the salt.

Add the rinsed rice to the pot and toast the rice, stirring constantly, until most of the liquid in the pot has been absorbed, 5 to 7 minutes.

Stir in the stock. Cover the pot with a towel or foil and then the lid, and reduce the heat to low so the mixture simmers. Cook, maintaining a simmer and gently stirring the rice at least twice, until the rice is tender, 20 to 25 minutes. Remove the bay leaves. Season to taste with salt. Fluff the rice and serve immediately. The jollof will keep in an airtight container in the refrigerator for up to 7 days.

Chichinga
(page 229)

Jollof Rice
(page 163)

Coconut Curry Chickpeas with
Mustard Greens (page 152)

Sweet Fried Plantains
with Benne Miso,
Benne Seeds, and
Onions (page 157)

CAROLINA GOLD RICE AND BUTTER

Serves 4

A plate or bowl of perfectly cooked rice is a luxury, and rice that is cooked with care is a gift. This recipe celebrates Anson Mills Carolina Gold rice, an heirloom rice variety that was once the most popular in the Americas, planted by enslaved Africans brought to southeastern states like South Carolina and Georgia. Carolina Gold is not the same stuff you see on supermarket shelves; this specific variety grown by Anson Mills is one of the best rice varieties in the country. Chef BJ Dennis, born and raised in South Carolina, taught me about rice and the role it plays in his life as a Gullah Geechee, and how it's deeply tied to his heritage as a descendant of Africans enslaved in South Carolina. When I heard him talk, it made me think about how much of a role rice has played in my life and the meals I've eaten as a Ghanaian American. This recipe honors Chef Dennis's ancestors who made it possible for this grain to thrive in the Americas.

4 cups water

1 cup Anson Mills Carolina Gold rice, rinsed and drained (see Note, page 151)

4 tablespoons (½ stick) unsalted butter, cut into small pieces

1 tablespoon fine sea salt, plus more to taste

Position a rack in the center of the oven and preheat the oven to 350°F. Line a rimmed baking sheet with parchment paper.

In a medium pot, combine the spring water, rice, 2 tablespoons of the butter, and the salt. Bring to a boil, then reduce the heat to medium-low, cover, and cook until just tender, 12 to 15 minutes. Using a colander, drain and rinse the rice under cool water to stop the cooking process.

Spread the rice out on the prepared baking sheet. Scatter the remaining 2 tablespoons of butter over the top and sprinkle with salt to taste. Bake until the rice is cooked through, about 12 minutes. Remove the rice from the oven, then fluff and serve hot.

WAAKYE RICE

Serves 6 to 8

I love calling waakye the "OG peas and rice dish." Whenever I land in Ghana, the first WhatsApp message I send is to Jay Gyebi, an entrepreneur and chef in Ghana who makes my favorite waakye, a delicious mess of spicy tomato sauce, rice, boiled eggs, and even spaghetti noodles. By the time I'm through customs and have checked into my hotel, it's waiting at the front desk for me. This recipe is for a fundamental part of the dish: the rice. It's a traditional version, so you really get a sense of the flavors. Pair this with Waakye Stew (page 95) and as many accompaniments as you like (see Note). You can order Ghanaian waakye leaves online.

2 cups dried sea island red peas or black-eyed peas, rinsed then soaked overnight in a few inches of cool water

2 garlic cloves, crushed

5 dried waakye leaves (millet/ sorghum leaves)

¼ teaspoon baking soda

2½ cups jasmine rice, rinsed and drained (see Note, page 151)

3 tablespoons virgin coconut oil

1 tablespoon kosher salt, plus more to taste

Drain and rinse the soaked peas thoroughly.

In a large pot, combine the peas, garlic, and 4½ cups of water. Bring to a simmer over medium heat and cook until the peas are about 80 percent done, 20 to 25 minutes. Drain the peas and remove the garlic, and set aside in the same pot.

Meanwhile, rinse the waakye leaves thoroughly. Place in a large pot with 3 cups of water and the baking soda. Bring to a boil over high heat and cook until the water is a deep red color, about 3 minutes. Remove from the heat and strain through a fine-mesh sieve, reserving the liquid and discarding the leaves. You should have 2½ cups of liquid.

Add the rice to the pot with the beans. Add 2 tablespoons of the coconut oil, the salt, and 2½ cups of the red waakye water. Stir well to combine, then bring to a boil over high heat. Reduce the heat to low, cover with a piece of parchment paper and the lid, and simmer gently until the rice is cooked through and all of the liquid is absorbed, about 17 minutes. Remove from the heat and let the rice steam, covered, for 5 minutes, then uncover and gently fluff. Add the remaining 1 tablespoon of coconut oil. Let the rice sit uncovered for 5 minutes. Season to taste with additional salt, if desired, before serving.

Note: Waakye rice is traditionally served with Waakye Stew (page 95), gari (for sourcing, see page 26), plain spaghetti, plantains, fried fish, and/or Shito (page 40), but you can combine or omit whichever components you wish.

PEAS AND RICE

Serves 6

Arguably one of the most popular dishes to come from the Caribbean, peas and rice reminds me so much of Waakye Rice (page 167) because of the ingredients and techniques that are used. Again, the commonalities between West African and Caribbean cooking are so apparent. This hearty side dish is flavored with fresh thyme, fruity notes from the allspice berries, and earthy kidney beans. Serve it with Oxtail Stew (page 221) for the ultimate Caribbean experience.

1 cup dried red kidney beans, rinsed then soaked overnight in a few inches of cool water

1 small red onion, finely diced

2 scallions, finely chopped (white and green parts)

2 sprigs of thyme

1 Scotch bonnet or habanero pepper, left whole

2 garlic cloves, crushed

2 teaspoons kosher salt

½ teaspoon freshly ground black pepper

½ teaspoon peeled and grated fresh ginger

1 (13.5-ounce) can full-fat coconut milk

2 teaspoons browning sauce

5 allspice berries

2 cups long-grain rice, rinsed and drained (see Note, page 151)

Drain the kidney beans. In a large saucepan, cover the beans with water by about 2 inches and bring to a boil over medium-high heat. Add the onion, scallions, thyme, whole Scotch bonnet, garlic, salt, black pepper, and ginger. Cook the kidney beans until they're tender and break easily between your fingers, about 20 minutes. (Depending on how well the beans are soaked, you may need more time for them to become tender. Add more water if necessary to keep the beans from drying out or burning.)

Remove and discard the Scotch bonnet pepper. Add the coconut milk, browning sauce, allspice berries, and rice. Stir thoroughly. There should be only about ½ inch of liquid above the beans and rice. If not, remove or add a little water to reach the correct level. Reduce the heat to medium-low. Cover the pan and cook, stirring every 5 to 7 minutes with a wooden spoon, until the rice is cooked through, about 30 minutes. Remove from the heat and allow to steam, covered, for 10 minutes before fluffing with a fork. Remove the thyme sprigs, then serve immediately. The rice will keep in an airtight container in the refrigerator for 1 week.

OMO TUO
Rice Balls

Serves 6

In many African homes, main courses come with the choice of fufu, kenkey, or omo tuo as the starch on the plate. These and many other starchy dumplings are called swallows and are delicious on their own and also make the perfect pairing for soups or stews. Swallows are traditionally meant to be eaten with your hands. There is a visceral connection between self and food when you're directly touching what you're eating. There is no fuss, you know exactly how hot your food is, and you never miss what you want to grab. This rice ball is just like it sounds: a mound of rice that is slightly sticky and formed into a ball. It's meant to be eaten with your hands as a vehicle for your main dish. It's a good introduction to swallows, and I actually prefer it sometimes to getting a plate of rice. No need to rinse your rice for this recipe; we actually want some of the rice's starch to help hold the ball together. Your finished product should be warm, moist, and easy to pick up.

2 cups long-grain white rice, such as jasmine or basmati

2 teaspoons kosher salt

In a medium pot, combine the rice, salt, and 3 cups of water and bring to a boil over high heat. Reduce the heat to medium-low and cook, covered, just as you would with a regular pot of rice, until most of the water is absorbed, 15 to 18 minutes.

Using a sturdy wooden spatula or banku ta, as it's called in Ghana, bring the rice toward the side of the pot, then turn it over (this is called the mash and fold method) to create more starch in the rice so it sticks together, adding a tablespoon of water if needed to form a soft, mushy consistency. Mash and fold consistently until the rice is uniformly soft and able to form into a ball.

Dampen a small bowl. Scoop a portion of the rice the size of an orange into the bowl and swirl it around the bowl using your fingers until the rice comes together into a smooth ball. Transfer to a plate and cover with a damp warm towel to keep the rice warm. Repeat with the remaining rice.

Serve warm with stews and soups. Omo tuo can be kept wrapped tightly in plastic wrap and refrigerated for up to 5 days.

BANKU

Serves 4

This is my favorite swallow that Ghana has to offer. Banku is a staple in the country and region and is typically eaten for lunch and dinner. The sticky dough is made from a mixture of corn and cassava flour that has been fermented, giving banku its signature sour taste. It's delicious as is, but it's taken to the next level when served with stews, soups, or sauces. Eating banku with Shito (page 40) and Whole Fried Tilapia (page 185) and various pepper sauces has been my personal go-to since I was a kid—and not much has changed. I also highly recommend you enjoy banku with groundnut soup (page 103) or palm nut soup (page 113). Always mix the dough thoroughly, and when cooking, be ready for a workout using the mash and fold method; this is where the banku ta (see page 32) enters the chat—to make light work of any pot of banku.

2 cups Fermented Banku Dough (recipe follows)   **1 teaspoon kosher salt**

In a medium heavy-bottomed pot over medium-low heat, combine the fermented dough with about 1 cup of water. Using a banku ta or wooden spatula, mix the dough and water until you have a creamy-smooth consistency (it's very important that you mix thoroughly here). You can help break down the dough by smearing it on the side of the pot. Once the mixture is smooth, increase the heat to medium-high and season with the salt. Begin stirring the mixture (it's crucial that you stir constantly to remove any lumps) until you feel resistance, 5 to 7 minutes. Once the mixture becomes thick, it's time for the mash and fold method. Continue to cook the banku while constantly bringing the mixture to the side of the pot. Using the flat side of your wooden spatula, smear, gather, and fold the banku on the side of the pot closest to you (you'll need a little elbow grease here), until you have a silky-smooth consistency, about 7 minutes. Reduce the heat as low as it will go. Add $^2/_3$ cup water and cover with a lid to steam the banku for 10 minutes. Remove the lid, then mash and fold again for 5 minutes to ensure a smooth consistency.

Turn off the heat and fill a small bowl with a bit of water. Take a ball of dough the size of an orange and place it in the bowl. Shape the banku by swirling it around the bowl with your fingers until you have a smooth, round dumpling shape. Repeat with the rest of the dough, making 8 balls. Serve warm.

Once cooled completely, the banku will keep covered in plastic wrap in the refrigerator for up to 1 week. To steam leftover banku, fill a large pot with water and place a fitted steamer over the top to cover, making sure the water doesn't touch the steamer, then bring to a boil over high heat. Place the banku on the steamer in a single layer, cover, and let steam for 15 minutes, until warmed through. Let cool for a few minutes before you handle the banku.

Recipe continues

Fermented Banku Dough
Makes 5½ cups

This dough takes a few days to ferment and can be a bit tricky to make, but once you have perfected the method, you'll be making it quite often.

3 cups corn flour   **2 cups cassava flour**

In a large bowl, combine the corn and cassava flours and mix until well combined. Gradually add ⅔ cup of warm water and mix using clean hands until thoroughly combined. The mixture should feel like wet sand, not too wet but able to hold its shape when squeezed. Pat the dough down into a large container, doing your best to remove any air pockets. Cover with plastic wrap that touches the surface of the dough. Place the container in a warm, dark spot for at least 2 days or up to 3 days (if you want a more fermented flavor), until you can smell a significant difference. The fermented dough will keep in an airtight container in the refrigerator for up to 1 week.

FUFU

Fufu holds a special place in the hearts of most Ghanaians. It's a dish that has been passed down through many generations, and I see it as a symbol of Ghanaian identity and heritage. Ghana is made up of over one hundred different ethnic groups, all with their own languages and subcultures. Fufu can be just as diverse as the people in the country, and depending on where you land in Ghana, the ingredients used to make this dish vary too. Typically the Ga tribe makes their fufu from cassava, and the Ewe tribe is known to make fufu from yam. For the Ashanti tribe, my family's lineage, fufu is typically made from a combination of boiled plantains and cassava. Making fufu traditionally is a very laborious task, and when done by expert hands, it can look like a professional sport. This recipe mimics some of that hard work but with a few home-cook hacks that make for a far easier time. Similar to the traditional technique, this fufu will eventually need to be mashed and folded into itself. The time and effort are well worth it because the end result is a supple, starchy dumpling that's the perfect vessel for your meal.

1 (1-pound) small cassava, peeled, woody center removed, and cubed

2 green plantains, peeled, cubed, and boiled (see Notes)

2 teaspoons kosher salt

The night before, or at least 4 hours prior to cooking, freeze the cubed cassava; this will make blending a whole lot easier once it's thawed.

When ready to cook, remove the cassava from the freezer and thaw at room temperature for 15 minutes. In a high-speed blender, combine the cassava, plantains, and 2 cups of water. Blend on high speed until you have a smooth puree; it should resemble a thick pancake batter. Pour the blended mixture into a large heavy-bottomed pot, stir in the salt, and set over medium heat. With a banku ta or wooden spatula, stir the mixture continuously until the dough is completely silky, up to 20 minutes. Once this consistency is reached, clean your wooden spatula of any built-up fufu and wet it. With the handle of the wet spoon, poke little holes down to the bottom of the pot and pour 1 teaspoon of water in each hole. Reduce the heat to medium-low, place the lid over the pot, and steam the fufu until it is smooth, sticky, and pliable, 15 to 20 minutes. Stir once more.

Dampen a small bowl with water. Scoop a portion of the fufu the size of an orange into the bowl and swirl it around using your fingers until the fufu comes together into a smooth ball. Transfer to a plate and repeat with the remaining fufu. Serve warm with stews and soups.

Notes: Boil plantains for 15 minutes or until fork-tender.

You can purchase fufu in powdered form. Follow the manufacturer's instructions to rehydrate.

SEAFOOD

Taking a Leap

During any formidable learning experience, there's often a moment where, along the lines of "woforo dua pa a" (see page 118), you have to trust the tree that you're climbing and step out on a branch on your way to the top. That branch may lead you farther up or collapse under your feet.

When I was still a sous chef for Marc Forgione, one day after work, I looked up chef Bryan Voltaggio's restaurant, Volt, in Frederick, Maryland. Like many people, I watched the sixth season of *Top Chef* and saw Chef Voltaggio and admired his stellar technique. When he and his brother released a cookbook, I bought it because I was such a fan. I followed his career from there, amazed by how talented and creative he was, and continues to be. I saw the company had posted an opening for a line cook. I stopped with my cursor on the page, excited for what felt like an opportunity to grow my skills. I had no idea how I was going to make this happen, but I knew I could figure it out. I sent in my résumé and was later called in to do a stage at the restaurant. So I made my way via train and then bus to Frederick.

A stage is a day, or a couple of days, where a line cook or chef works in a restaurant kitchen to see if they're a good fit. It's really a time for you as a cook to figure out if you like the team, like the kitchen, like the menu. The team there is evaluating you as well and seeing if you'll be a suitable match. I showed up, eager to show off my skills and potentially meet Chef Voltaggio, but found out he was in India for work and wasn't going to be around. After the stage, I headed back to New York, thinking about my next steps and what I wanted to do with my career.

On the Greyhound bus ride home, I called my sister to catch up and to update her on how my stage went. I tried to convey a sense of optimism to her, but my voice betrayed me. She could hear more than I was letting on, knowing I was still curious about traveling and seeing more of the world. She listened to me and said, "How crazy would it be if you moved to London and got your master's?" Thinking I was in a rut, I had dreamed up the same idea before that trip to Maryland. (I now know that I wasn't in a rut; I was just learning the ropes of a hard industry and frustrated.) We talked a little more about how I should follow my interests in nutrition and food and pursue an education in public health. As the bus hurried back to Port Authority in Manhattan, I mulled it over in my head, excited by the idea of going back to school.

The next day I got a phone call from a number with a Maryland area code. It was Chef Voltaggio himself calling to officially offer me the job. He was also calling to apologize for things being so hectic and not really having the time to sit down and chat with me, which was such a nice gesture. As much as I was a fan, I knew I had to step out onto another limb of the tree. I thought back to my conversation with my sister just the day before.

I took a deep breath and told Chef Voltaggio, one of my culinary idols, that my plans had changed and that I had decided I was going to go get a master's degree instead. He gave me his blessing and congratulated me on the decision.

By that summer I was scouting colleges in England and Scotland, and ultimately landed at the University of Westminster to study international public health. It was an easy choice because I have family in London. I was moving far away, but to a place where I had a small network of people I could rely on.

Sometimes I think about what my life would look like if I had taken that job at Volt instead of going to grad school. I think something good would have come of it, and I would have learned a lot, but grad school forced me to slow down and think about what I wanted to do and, more importantly, why I wanted to do it.

That time in London, and the degree I earned, changed my life and set me up for the next chapter once I moved back to the States. Knowing that I had taken a leap of faith and continued to climb the branches of the tree gave me the support to continue climbing to reach my goals. And it gave me a foundation for one of the biggest risks I've taken in my career.

GARLICKY GRILLED PRAWNS
with Chermoula

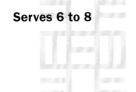

Serves 6 to 8

Grilling is the favored technique to cook these crustaceans practically everywhere on the African continent. In Ghana, the aroma of prawns charring over charcoal is a sensory experience that locals are lucky to encounter every day, and one that visitors are immediately drawn to once they arrive. It's not uncommon for grilled prawns to be cooked with garlic, citrus, and spices, but my take also features Africa's herby condiment of choice: chermoula. Sop up the prawns with garlicky melted butter and a little chermoula for the perfect bite. It's an herbaceous bomb with beautiful notes of ginger, citrus, and smoke from the grill. Serve the prawns as a snack or really impress a crowd by featuring this at your next dinner party.

Garlic Sauce

6 tablespoons unsalted butter, diced

2 tablespoons high-quality extra-virgin olive oil

¼ cup (packed) garlic cloves, minced

1 (½-inch) piece of fresh ginger, minced

2 teaspoons kosher salt, or more to taste

1½ tablespoons Mom's Hot Pepper Sauce (page 43) or store-bought Scotch bonnet hot sauce

1 tablespoon All-Day Seasoning Blend (page 35)

½ tablespoon grated lime zest

1 tablespoon fresh lime juice, or more to taste

2 teaspoons (packed) light brown sugar

2 teaspoons fish sauce

Prawns

24 to 36 king or tiger prawns, peeled and deveined (see Note, page 184)

2 tablespoons high-quality extra-virgin olive oil

1 tablespoon All-Day Seasoning Blend (page 35)

2 teaspoons kosher salt

1½ teaspoons sweet paprika

1 teaspoon freshly ground black pepper

⅛ teaspoon cayenne pepper

Sliced sourdough bread

3 tablespoons Chermoula (recipe follows), for serving

Special Equipment

12 to 16 skewers (if using wooden skewers, soak in water for 40 minutes before grilling)

Preheat an outdoor grill to high heat for 20 minutes or a grill pan over medium-high heat for 10 minutes.

Make the garlic sauce: In a large saucepan (large enough to hold all of the sauce and shrimp once cooked), melt the butter and oil over medium-high heat. Add the garlic, ginger, and salt. Stir until the garlic and ginger are light golden brown, 40 seconds to 1 minute. Immediately remove from the heat, then stir in the hot pepper sauce, seasoning blend, lime zest, lime juice, brown sugar, and fish sauce. Season with more salt and lime juice, if desired, and keep warm.

Make the prawns: Using paper towels, dab the prawns to dry and remove any excess moisture, then place in a large bowl. Add the olive oil, seasoning blend, salt, paprika, black pepper, and cayenne and toss to coat the prawns.

Recipe continues

Thread 2 or 3 prawns onto each skewer. Grill the prawns until pink and opaque, about 3 minutes per side. As the prawns finish, remove them from the skewer, add them to the pan with the sauce, and toss to coat well. Lightly grill the bread on both sides for 2 minutes.

Spread the chermoula on a serving platter, top with the prawns and sauce, and serve with the toasted sourdough bread.

Note: If your prawns haven't been deveined, use a sharp knife to make a long incision down the length of the back, then remove the vein.

Chermoula
Makes 1½ cups

Chermoula is a tangy, aromatic, and slightly spicy sauce that originated in North Africa and is the perfect accompaniment to the shrimp here.

1 cup (packed) fresh flat-leaf parsley leaves and tender stems, finely chopped

1 tablespoon (packed) fresh oregano leaves, finely chopped

1 tablespoon minced garlic

½ tablespoon lemon zest

½ tablespoon orange zest

1½ tablespoons fresh lemon juice, or more to taste

1 tablespoon fresh orange juice

1 tablespoon champagne vinegar or apple cider vinegar

½ tablespoon smoked paprika

½ teaspoon ground cumin

⅛ teaspoon cayenne pepper

6 tablespoons high-quality extra-virgin olive oil

¼ cup finely chopped shallot

1 teaspoon kosher salt, or more to taste

In a medium bowl, mix the parsley, oregano, and garlic. (You should have about 1 packed cup finely chopped herbs.) Stir in the lemon zest, orange zest, lemon juice, orange juice, vinegar, paprika, cumin, and cayenne. Slowly whisk in the olive oil. Stir in the shallot. Season with the salt. Taste and add more salt or lemon juice to taste, if desired.

Serve right away. The chermoula will keep in an airtight container in the refrigerator for 1 day.

WHOLE FRIED TILAPIA

Serves 2

You'll see tilapia on menus in many parts of West Africa because its meaty flesh and neutral flavor are perfect for both frying and grilling. Without a doubt, freshwater tilapia is the most commonly eaten fish in Ghana. The country produces and consumes its own tilapia, meaning it's much fresher than what we can get here in the States, where tilapia often gets a bad rap because a lot of it is imported. Fried tilapia is served in so many ways, but in this book, I recommend it with a spread of shito and yam chips. You could also serve a swallow like Banku (page 173) or combine it with other dishes such as the Paw Paw Salad (page 133) or Jollof Rice (page 163) to get the same feel. This recipe is a traditional take on a fried tilapia, but feel free to fire up your grill instead, using the same marinade (see Note), or try it with red snapper.

2 tablespoons All-Day Seasoning Blend (page 35)

2 tablespoons ginger garlic puree, homemade (page 35) or store-bought

2 tablespoons Mom's Hot Pepper Sauce (page 43) or store-bought Scotch bonnet hot sauce

¼ teaspoon ground white pepper

¼ teaspoon kosher salt

1 (2½-pound) freshwater tilapia or red snapper, scaled, cleaned, gutted, and fins removed

Peanut oil or other neutral oil, for frying

2 large sprigs of rosemary

1 sprig of thyme

Shito (page 40) or Green Shito (page 40), for serving

Puna Yam Chips (page 76), for serving

In a small bowl, combine the seasoning blend, ginger garlic puree, hot pepper sauce, white pepper, and salt and mix well to make a paste.

Pat the fish very dry inside and out using paper towels. Using a sharp knife, score a crosshatch pattern into the fish, cutting deep enough to just expose the flesh but not break any bones. Rub the spice paste all over the fish, gently massaging it into the incisions and inside the cavity. Transfer to a plate. Let marinate at room temperature for 30 minutes or preferably overnight in the refrigerator, loosely covered with plastic wrap. If refrigerating overnight, let the fish come to room temperature before frying.

In a deep, heavy pot wide enough to hold the whole fish, add enough oil to come at least 1½ inches up the side of the pot. Heat the oil over medium-high heat until it registers 350°F on a deep-fry thermometer. Line a large plate or platter with paper towels.

Using paper towels, pat the fish dry, leaving some of the marinade on, and then fill its cavity with the rosemary and thyme. Close the fish carefully. (You can even close it using butcher's twine if you prefer.)

Carefully lower the fish into the hot oil until it is fully submerged. Fry until starting to turn crisp and golden, 3 to 5 minutes. Carefully flip the fish and fry until evenly golden brown all over, 3 to 5 minutes more. Using a fish spatula, transfer to the prepared platter to drain.

Serve immediately, with either classic or green shito, and yam chips.

Note: If you decide to grill the fish instead, prepare, marinate, and stuff the fish the same way. Preheat an outdoor grill to high heat and grill until you reach an internal temperature of 145°F and the fish is golden brown, 25 minutes total.

PAN-SEARED GROUPER
with Fried Peanut Salsa

Serves 2

During the pandemic in 2020, I was hired by Blue Chip Hospitality Group from Ghana to help open a restaurant called East End Bistro in the Osu area of Accra. Among other duties, creating a menu and training a new kitchen staff were my primary responsibilities. I developed this fried peanut salsa as a signature condiment for a few items from the menu—one of which was a simple pan-seared grouper.

Fried Peanut Salsa

½ cup peanut oil

2 tablespoons unsalted raw peanuts or groundnuts (for sourcing, see page 26)

¼ cup (loosely packed) fresh cilantro leaves, chopped

¼ cup (loosely packed) fresh curly parsley leaves, chopped

1 bunch chives, finely chopped

3 scallions, finely chopped (white and green parts)

1 small shallot, minced

1 jalapeño pepper, stemmed, seeded, and finely chopped

Juice of 1 lime, plus more to taste

2 garlic cloves, minced

1 tablespoon fresh oregano leaves, finely chopped

1 tablespoon red wine vinegar

1 teaspoon crushed red pepper flakes

½ teaspoon kosher salt, plus more to taste

½ teaspoon freshly ground black pepper

¼ cup high-quality extra-virgin olive oil

Grouper

2 (8-ounce) grouper fillets or other firm white fish, skin removed

1 tablespoon all-purpose flour

Kosher salt and freshly ground black pepper

1 tablespoon high-quality extra-virgin olive oil

2 tablespoons unsalted butter

Juice of ½ lemon

Make the fried peanut salsa: Line a plate with paper towels. In a small pot over medium heat, heat the peanut oil. When the oil is shimmering, fry the peanuts until golden, 5 to 7 minutes. Use a slotted spoon to carefully transfer the peanuts to the prepared plate to drain. (Alternatively, you can roast the peanuts on a small baking sheet in a 350°F oven until golden, 15 minutes.)

In an asanka or a mortar and pestle, crush the peanuts until they're crumbly. In a small bowl, mix the peanuts, cilantro, parsley, chives, scallions, shallot, jalapeño, lime juice, garlic, oregano, vinegar, red pepper flakes, salt, and black pepper. Whisk the salsa while drizzling in the olive oil until well combined, and season with more salt and lime juice to taste. Set aside. The salsa can be refrigerated in an airtight container for 10 days.

Make the grouper: With a paper towel, pat the fillets dry. Dust with the flour, then shake off any excess. Sprinkle on both sides with salt and pepper. Line a plate with paper towels.

In a medium sauté pan over medium-high heat, heat the olive oil and 1 tablespoon of the butter. When the butter is melted and bubbling, place the fillets in the pan and cook, undisturbed, for 3 to 4 minutes. Carefully slide a fish spatula under the fish, and if it releases without sticking, it's ready to flip. If the fillets won't release, give them another 30 seconds and try again. Add the remaining 1 tablespoon of butter and the lemon juice, then cook on the second side while basting with the lemon butter until crispy and golden brown, 2 to 3 minutes. Remove the fish from the pan and transfer to the paper towels to remove any excess oil. Serve the grouper topped with the salsa.

FRIED SARDINES
with Mom's Pepper Sauce

Serves 4 to 6

Sardines are a heavy favorite throughout West Africa and the Caribbean islands. They remind me of the common throughlines that make the cooking practices and food of African descendants unique to parts of the world unfamiliar with their cuisines. Some of those practices can be seen even in a simply prepared dish like this one, from the frying and grilling techniques to the steps taken to season our food. From my knowledge and experience, if they're not from a can, fresh sardines are primarily either fried or grilled. I've had both, in Ghana, Jamaica, Bermuda, the Bahamas, and Barbados, which speaks to how similar our diets are and how versatile this ingredient is.

2 pounds sardines or other small fish such as anchovies or herring

2 lemons, 1 cut in half, 1 cut into wedges for serving

¼ cup green seasoning, homemade (page 36) or store-bought

2 teaspoons kosher salt

1 teaspoon freshly ground black pepper

3 cups neutral oil, for frying (optional)

1 cup all-purpose flour (optional)

Mom's Hot Pepper Sauce (page 43), for serving

Clean the sardines by placing them on a cutting board and using a sharp paring knife to scrape off the scales. Once the scales are removed, rinse the sardines under cold water to wash away any loose scales or debris.

Fill a small bowl with cold water and squeeze the juice of 1 lemon in it. With a knife, make a shallow incision along the belly of a fish from the head to the tail. Gently open the belly and remove the innards and organs (you can use your fingers for this). Place the fish in the lemon water and rinse well to remove any impurities from the inside. Transfer the fish to a colander to drain and repeat with the remaining fish. Rinse the bowl. Place the sardines back in the bowl and season with the green seasoning, salt, and pepper. Transfer the sardines to an airtight container and marinate in the refrigerator for at least 4 hours or preferably overnight.

When ready to cook, remove the sardines from the refrigerator and bring to room temperature. You can either fry or grill the fish:

If frying, heat the oil in a deep, wide frying pan over medium heat. The oil is ready when it begins shimmering. Line a baking sheet with paper towels.

Put the flour in a shallow dish, then dip a fish in the flour, shake off the excess, and place carefully in the hot oil. Repeat with a few more sardines. Taking care not to crowd the pan, fry the sardines in batches, flipping them over a few times, until fully cooked and golden brown, about 8 minutes total. Using tongs, remove the fish and place on the prepared baking sheet to soak up any excess oil. Repeat with the remaining fish.

If grilling, omit the frying oil and flour. Preheat an outdoor grill to high. Grill the sardines until well charred on one side, 2 to 3 minutes. Using a metal spatula, flip the sardines over and grill until charred on the second side and cooked through, about 2 minutes longer.

Serve right away with hot pepper sauce and lemon wedges.

SALTED COD FRITTERS
with Anchovy Aioli

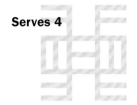

Serves 4

A lot of iconic West African dishes get their unique flavor profile from salted, cured, or smoked fish such as momoni (salted fermented fish), koobi (salted and dried tilapia), and of course salted cod. I like to think this practice of curing fish came from the Portuguese during the slave trade and that strong culinary influence migrated across the ocean to the waters of the Caribbean. Salted cod, or bacalhau in Portuguese, is the base of this dish. In the Caribbean, salted cod fritters are eaten as an appetizer or with a Sunday morning breakfast. This is a traditional take on the fritter with a little liberty taken on the anchovy aioli, which is meant to double down on the oceanic umami. As with most salted fish dishes, the magic is in the preparation: the cod needs to be soaked and rinsed to eliminate most of its salt content, so take your time on that step.

Fritters

8 ounces salted boneless cod

1 cup all-purpose flour, plus more for dusting

2 teaspoons baking powder

2 teaspoons All-Day Seasoning Blend (page 35)

½ teaspoon (packed) light brown sugar

Freshly ground black pepper

½ medium yellow onion, finely diced

1 large egg

3 tablespoons (loosely packed) finely chopped fresh flat-leaf parsley leaves

1 teaspoon finely chopped fresh thyme leaves

1 teaspoon Mom's Hot Pepper Sauce (page 43) or store-bought Scotch bonnet hot sauce

⅓ to ½ cup whole milk, as needed

Anchovy Aioli

6 oil-packed anchovies

1 garlic clove, coarsely chopped

2 tablespoons fresh lemon juice, plus more to taste

2 large egg yolks

1 teaspoon Dijon mustard

Kosher salt and freshly ground black pepper

½ cup neutral oil

1 tablespoon finely chopped fresh chives

1 tablespoon finely chopped fresh tarragon leaves

1 tablespoon finely chopped fresh dill

1 tablespoon finely grated Parmesan cheese

3 cups neutral oil, for frying, plus more as needed

Prep the fritters: In a medium bowl, cover the salted cod with cold water. Soak in the refrigerator at least overnight and up to 3 days, changing the water every 12 hours, until the cod is free of its salty coating and softened enough to be able to be torn apart by hand.

Meanwhile, drain the fish, rinse with cold water, and break into chunks. Place in the bowl of a food processor and pulse until finely shredded.

In a medium bowl, whisk together the flour, baking powder, seasoning blend, brown sugar, and a pinch of pepper. Add the shredded fish, onion, egg, parsley, thyme, and hot pepper sauce. Using a rubber spatula, stir until well combined, then slowly stir in ⅓ cup milk, continuing to stir until a thick dough forms that holds together in a ball and adding more milk as needed a splash at a time to help the dough come together. Set the dough aside while you make the anchovy aioli.

Recipe continues

Make the anchovy aioli: In a mini food processor or blender, blitz the anchovies and garlic to form a paste. With the motor running, add the lemon juice, egg yolks, mustard, and salt and pepper to taste. Very gradually add the oil, drop by drop, with the motor still running, until the sauce has thickened and emulsified. (If using a mini food processor without an opening, add the oil tablespoon by tablespoon, blitzing until emulsified after each addition.) Transfer the mixture to a small bowl and fold in the chives, tarragon, dill, and Parmesan. If the mixture is too thick, add water 1 tablespoon at a time until the aioli is a consistency that can be drizzled. Taste for seasoning and add more lemon juice, if you like. Set aside while you fry the fritters.

Fry the fritters: In a medium, heavy, deep-sided skillet or Dutch oven, heat the oil to 350°F over medium heat. Line a platter with paper towels.

When the oil is hot, test the dough by dropping in a tiny spoonful of the cod mixture and frying until crisp and golden brown. When cool enough to handle, taste, then adjust the seasoning of the cod mixture as necessary.

Working in batches, drop tablespoon-size portions of dough into the hot oil and fry, turning occasionally, until the fritters are crisp and golden brown on all sides, 3 to 4 minutes. Use a slotted spoon to transfer the fritters to the prepared platter to drain.

Serve the fritters immediately with the anchovy aioli on the side for dipping.

LOBSTER
with Harissa Butter

Serves 4

Like many, I've always associated eating lobster with opulence or special occasions. Being raised in New York, whenever I would eat lobster, I knew that it came from the cold waters of the North Atlantic, considered to be the source of some of the tastiest lobster in the world. Through traveling in my career, I've actually found that I prefer the flavor of the spiny or rock lobster because they're smaller and more concentrated in flavor. These days, I work more often with this variety, which is primarily found in warmer Atlantic waters, whether along the shores of South Africa or the Caribbean Sea. Whichever you choose, American or spiny lobster, I truly believe that this crustacean doesn't need much help to taste amazing. The spicy tang of harissa paste, a North African condiment, helps amplify what's already very delicious. Fire up the grill or broiler for this recipe and enjoy.

Harissa Butter

½ cup (1 stick) unsalted butter, at room temperature

¼ cup harissa paste (I like Dea Harissa)

¼ cup finely chopped fresh curly parsley

1 tablespoon minced shallot

Zest of 1 lemon

1 tablespoon fresh lemon juice

½ tablespoon crushed red pepper flakes

4 garlic cloves, finely minced

Kosher salt and freshly ground black pepper

Breadcrumbs

6 tablespoons unsalted butter

1 tablespoon harissa paste

½ cup panko breadcrumbs

1 bunch chives, finely chopped

Kosher salt

Lobster

Kosher salt

4 (1- to 1½-pound) live lobsters

½ cup Pickled Red Onion (page 130), for garnish

½ small bunch chives, chopped, for garnish

Preheat an outdoor grill to medium-high heat (425°F) with the lid closed for 15 minutes. If using a broiler, preheat to high.

While the grill or broiler preheats, make the harissa butter: In a medium bowl, combine the softened butter, harissa paste, parsley, shallot, lemon zest, lemon juice, red pepper flakes, and garlic. Whisk until smooth, then season with salt and black pepper. Set aside.

Make the breadcrumbs: In a medium sauté pan over medium heat, add the butter and harissa paste. Cook, swirling the pan around, until the harissa is caramelized, 3 to 5 minutes. Add the panko and cook, stirring constantly, until the breadcrumbs are browned, 4 to 6 minutes. Immediately transfer to a medium bowl, then stir in the chives and season with salt. Set aside.

Make the lobster: Fill a large lidded pot with water and bring to a boil over high heat. While the water boils, prepare an ice bath in a large bowl. Salt the boiling water generously, then add the lobsters to the pot head-first. Cover the pot and cook until the lobsters are bright red, 2 minutes. Transfer to the prepared ice bath to shock, about 3 minutes, then remove the lobsters.

Recipe continues

Using a cleaver or large chef's knife, split each shocked lobster in half lengthwise through its head and tail; the lobsters will not be cooked all the way through. Scoop out and discard the yellow-green tomalley and break off the claws. Transfer the lobster halves, cut-side up, to a baking sheet; crack the claws using the back of a knife, a lobster cracker, or a crab mallet and place them on the baking sheet as well.

Place the lobster halves on the grill grates, cut-side down, and cook until grill marks appear, 4 minutes. Carefully turn over and spoon about 2 teaspoons of the harissa butter onto each lobster half. As the butter begins to melt, use a brush to baste all over the flesh. Continue grilling until the meat is cooked through and coated in melted butter, 4 to 5 minutes more. Remove the tails from the grill and repeat with the claws.

To serve, transfer the tails and claws to a platter. Layer the inside of each lobster tail half with breadcrumbs, then garnish both the halves and claws with pickled red onion and chives.

OYSTERS
with Hibiscus Mignonette and Pickled Ginger

Makes 12 oysters

During the time I was on *Top Chef,* we had an elimination challenge to create a dish that mimicked the flavors of a classic cocktail and could be served during a busy cocktail reception. I chose The Last Word as my cocktail and raw oysters with mignonette as my dish for two reasons: 1) adding a brininess to the flavors of a sweet, anise-spiced cocktail sounded delicious and 2) because it was perfect for the setting. My instinct was right, and I won that challenge. When I got home after competing, I had a very similar task at hand for a wedding reception where the couple, a bride from Nigeria and a groom from Ghana, had requested that the food for their celebration be based on popular West African dishes. As I was just coming off the heels of *Top Chef,* an oyster inspired by the ingredients in Sobolo (page 89) was where my mind went for the same two reasons. These oysters were a huge hit during that reception, and I think you'll love them too.

Mignonette

¼ cup dried hibiscus blossoms

½ cup red wine vinegar

1 tablespoon fresh orange juice

1 tablespoon (packed) minced shallot

¼ teaspoon freshly ground black pepper

12 large oysters, shucked and released from the shell (see Note)

2 teaspoons store-bought pickled ginger, finely diced, for serving

Make the mignonette: In a small bowl, soak the hibiscus in the vinegar and orange juice for 15 minutes. Strain the mixture through a small fine-mesh sieve into a small bowl, pressing on the hibiscus to extract as much liquid as possible. Discard the hibiscus. Add the shallot and pepper to the vinegar mixture.

Spoon a bit of mignonette onto each of the oysters, top with a little pickled ginger, and serve immediately.

Note: If you are shucking your own oysters, scrub them under cold running water to remove any visible dirt. Over a cutting board, set the oyster belly-side down on a folded towel, with the hinge (the area where the shells taper together) facing your dominant hand. Fold the towel over the oyster to expose only the hinge, and place your nondominant hand over the top of the covered oyster to hold it in place. Using an oyster knife, carefully search for the center point of the hinge with your knife's tip so it can have some leverage. Once the tip of the knife is in the hinge's center point, wiggle the knife around until you feel that the shell has popped open; you may need to twist your knife sideways to pry the shell open. Carefully remove the top shell and discard. Using your oyster knife, remove the oyster from its connecting adductor muscle by sweeping your knife underneath the oyster to release it from the shell.

CRAB FRIED RICE
with Benne Miso and Scallions

Serves 4

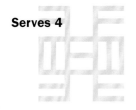

Before there were any major Western fast-food restaurants in Ghana, one of the only options that was available in Accra came from Papaye, a distinctively West African fast-food chain that specializes in local versions of classic international dishes—one of which is fried rice. Fried rice is seen as an East Asian dish, but today fried rice in Ghana is as much a part of the food culture as any traditional African rice dish. Fried rice is made for all special occasions and is easily adaptable, so it's a staple in my kitchen. I use benne seed miso from Keepwell Vinegar for a funky umami flavor, which I enjoy. This version is made with crab, but feel free to substitute whatever seafood you have available.

3 tablespoons peanut oil or neutral oil

½ medium yellow onion, chopped

2 large garlic cloves, finely chopped

1 (½-inch) piece of fresh ginger, peeled and finely chopped

4 scallions, coarsely chopped (white and green parts)

2 large eggs, beaten

3½ cups cooked white rice, cold or at room temperature

2 tablespoons soy sauce

1 tablespoon oyster sauce

1½ tablespoons benne miso (for sourcing, see page 25) or red miso

¾ cup crabmeat (lump or backfin), picked through

2 teaspoons benne seeds (for sourcing, see page 25) or sesame seeds

Kosher salt

Chili crisp, for serving (optional)

In a wok or large sauté pan, heat the oil over medium-high heat. When the oil starts shimmering (after about a minute), add the onion and sauté, stirring frequently, until fragrant, 1 to 2 minutes. Add the garlic, ginger, and half of the scallions and continue to cook, stirring constantly, until fragrant, another 2 minutes.

Move the aromatics to the edges of the wok to create a circle in the middle of the pan. Add the eggs to the center and allow the eggs to set for 10 seconds before stirring with a spatula to create curds. Immediately add the rice, soy sauce, oyster sauce, and miso and mix with the eggs and vegetables on the side of the wok. Cook, stirring frequently, until well combined, about 7 minutes, then add 1 tablespoon of water. Continue to cook, stirring frequently, until the rice is fully coated, another 2 minutes. Add the crab, remaining scallions, benne seeds, and salt to taste and stir to combine.

Divide the fried rice among 4 plates and serve immediately, topped with chili crisp if you like.

BIRDS AND MEATS

A National Stage

Standing in the dining room of the Muhammad Ali Center in Louisville, Kentucky, was a surreal experience. It was 2018, and I was a contestant on *Top Chef: Kentucky.* For that day's challenge we had to make a dish that spoke to Muhammad Ali's incredible legacy as part of a six-course progressive dinner.

We were down to six contestants from fifteen. I wanted to stand out and make something that epitomized West Africa and the techniques and flavors that have had such an enormous impact on me. To add to the pressure, the guest judge for the episode was Ali's daughter, Laila Ali, a famous boxer and philanthropist in her own right. I chose to make fufu and red sauce, a dish that any Ghanaian and African would know, with the red sauce inspired by Ali's famous "Rumble in the Jungle" fight, which took place in what is now the Democratic Republic of the Congo.

Getting to serve the judges and the dining room of guests this unmistakably African dish, one that's usually eaten with your hands, and highlighting ingredients like cassava and plantain that are integral to the cuisines of the continent, was quite literally a dream come true: months prior to joining the competition I had a dream that I served Padma Lakshmi and Tom Colicchio cassava and plantain fufu. It was something I knew I had to do if I ever got a chance to be on the show.

After receiving my master's degree in London in 2013, I had moved back to the States and started working at Harlem Children's Zone, creating lesson plans for middle and high school–aged children to teach them the basics of cooking. It was great, but I missed professional kitchens, so I began working at a restaurant called the Red Rabbit in Manhattan. When I wasn't at work, I was watching *Top Chef,* dreaming of being part of the show one day and sharing my story on that platform.

I obviously thought being on the show would be a good move to help showcase myself and my talents, but beyond that, and bigger than that, it would be a way to continue to highlight the cooking of West Africa and the continent at large. It was wild to me that in fifteen seasons there hadn't been a contestant from Ghana or one who specialized in the various cuisines of Africa. I thought that was unacceptable. Africa is the second-biggest continent in the world, yet African food is so unknown. I felt it was an opportunity to show how West African cooking techniques and practices are on a par with any other cuisine my fellow competitors might be cooking.

In 2017, after working in restaurants and running Pinch and Plate, a mobile catering service that produced dinner parties around Washington, D.C., I auditioned for *Top Chef.* Competing was grueling, and to make things even more intense, Janell was pregnant with our daughter, Lennox, meaning I could become a father at any moment. I was focused on winning because it would impact our lives for the better, but it was hard not to think about Janell and our baby. I poured my focus and love into doing my best on the show and winning the challenges that they threw at us.

My focus was paying off. That night in the Muhammad Ali Center, watching Padma Lakshmi and Tom Colicchio eat fufu and red sauce, and getting to speak to Laila Ali, was such a motivator to continue cooking this food and telling my story. I could see how diners engaged with the story behind the food, as well as the fact that the food was delicious. Those connections kept me in the competition week after week.

Waking up in Macau as a finalist was such a beautiful moment, but it was still filled with nerves and anxiety because I had to cook the best meal of my life. I chose to tell the story of the transatlantic slave trade and how forced migration of Africans can be traced through flavors, ingredients, and techniques that have touched the world. The show broke the final competition into two parts: the first part had the final three contestants (Kelsey Barnard Clark, Sara Bradley, and myself) serve the first course of our four-course meal. The chef with the least favorite dish would be eliminated, while the other two would be able to continue on with their remaining three courses.

I would start with a steak tartare with egg yolk sauce, flavoring the tender cubes of meat with a paste made with the same ingredients as the rub that makes Jamaican jerk so flavorful: allspice, cinnamon, nutmeg, Scotch bonnet. For the second dish I wanted to make a lobster yassa, a play on the famous Senegalese dish usually made with chicken and onions cooked down into an almost jam-like consistency. I would follow that up with short ribs with cassava shows how new-world ingredients work really well with traditional African starches like cassava. And for the dessert, a simple hibiscus sorbet. In each course I wanted to demonstrate the versatility and modernity that can be found in African ingredients and hopefully show the judges that so many of the flavors that are paramount to the continent are ones they already know. I wanted to put those tastes on blast, and smack the judges in the face with flavor.

That day I got to serve only my first dish, the steak tartare. The lotus chips that I wanted to serve as a crispy accompaniment to my tartare were too dark and inconsistent, and the judges felt they couldn't taste the beef alongside the jerk. I was sent home and didn't get to finish the story I had so carefully planned out.

It's hard to describe just how crushing it was to go home at that point. On the way out of the hotel in Macau, I ran into the guest judge for the finale, chef Alexander Smalls. I gave him a hug and nearly collapsed into his arms. "I tried to hold out," I said to him. I was devastated that I wouldn't get to cook this meal exploring the contributions of enslaved Africans, a story Chef Smalls has examined in his writing and his work as a restaurateur. I was walking away from the competition, but there was more meat on the bone, more story to tell, and more of myself to show.

What I couldn't predict was what would happen after the finale aired. Over the course of the season, people from Ghana, West Africa, and all over the world had started reaching out, tagging me, sending messages saying they were so proud to see someone cooking this food on television. When the finale aired, people voiced how upset they were that I was cut. Fans of the show even began calling me "The People's Champ," noting how I was cooking food that felt familiar for so many. It was flattering, but it also made me realize how hungry people are for stories about the continent. I think the biggest takeaway for me was the feeling that I'm on the right path. Cooking food from the African diaspora and winning with those dishes was the validation I needed to continue.

Not too long after the season ended, Tom Colicchio invited me to host a dinner at his restaurant, Craft, in New York City, to finish telling the story I had started on the show. That evening I served all four courses, combining the flavors of West Africa, the Caribbean, the American South, and Brazil into a narrative that captured not only the breadth of flavor and complexity found in these cuisines but also the lasting connections between all of the places that the slave trade touched. I was back in my hometown, and my mom was in attendance. I got to tell my story in the *Washington Post* and the *New York Times*. I thought finishing the meal would feel like closing the chapter, but it was only the beginning. That meat was still there on the bone, and there are connections still to be explored from all the lands the slave trade touched. That's what I'm exploring with my cooking, and this still, somehow, feels like the beginning.

AKƆMFƐM (GUINEA FOWL)
with Suya, Pickled Onion, and Charred Tomatoes

Serves 4

We don't cook much guinea fowl in America, but in West Africa, where the bird is native, it's one of the most popular proteins. Guinea fowl is a game bird, which means it roams wild, eating a diverse diet of greens and insects. It doesn't taste very gamy, but the noticeable difference is in the texture of the meat, which I prefer over your standard chicken. Because guinea fowl is truly free-range, its flesh is leaner, darker, and meatier. This recipe calls for the bird to be spatchcocked over a grill, which will allow for a quicker cook time, preventing the lean meat from drying out quickly. Marinated and seasoned with suya, then served with onion and tomatoes, this is a tribute to authentic Ghanaian street food that tastes like you're there.

Guinea Fowl

1 (3- to 5-pound) guinea fowl, spatchcocked (see Note, page 208)

1 lemon, cut in half

1 medium red onion, grated on the large holes of a box grater

3 to 5 tablespoons Suya Spice Blend (page 35), as needed

2 tablespoons All-Day Seasoning Blend (page 35)

2 teaspoons kosher salt

Suya Paste

3 tablespoons Suya Spice Blend (page 35)

2 tablespoons peanut oil

1 tablespoon red wine vinegar

1 teaspoon kosher salt

Charred Tomatoes

1 pound cherry tomatoes or grape tomatoes

1 tablespoon high-quality extra-virgin olive oil

½ teaspoon kosher salt, plus more to taste

¼ teaspoon freshly ground black pepper, plus more to taste

3 sprigs of thyme

Pickled Onion

1 small to medium yellow onion, thinly sliced

1 cup Pickling Liquid (page 43), hot

Prepare the guinea fowl: At least 2 hours or up to 2 days before cooking, place the guinea fowl in a large baking dish or bowl—it should comfortably hold the flattened bird. Rub the cut sides of the lemon all over the guinea fowl, then rinse the bird thoroughly under cold water. Pat very dry with paper towels. Return the guinea fowl to the dish and cover with grated red onion, making sure it is coated evenly. Sprinkle evenly with suya, seasoning blend, and salt, then rub all over the bird. (The guinea fowl should be fully and generously coated with the spice, so add a little more suya if needed.) Cover with plastic wrap and allow to marinate in the refrigerator for at least 2 hours or (ideally) up to 2 days.

When you're ready to cook, preheat an outdoor grill to 375°F (or medium-high heat) for indirect grilling. Remove the guinea fowl from the refrigerator and allow to come to room temperature.

Make the suya paste: In a small bowl, mix the suya, peanut oil, vinegar, salt, and 1 tablespoon of water.

Recipe continues

Position the bird skin-side up over indirect heat and place a cast-iron pan, brick wrapped in foil, or something else heatproof and heavy on the bird to ensure even cooking and that it stays flat. Grill, brushing with the suya paste every 10 to 15 minutes and turning over once during cooking, until the internal temperature reaches 150°F in the thickest part of the thigh, 40 to 50 minutes. Move the bird over direct heat, basting once more with the suya paste, to char, about 5 minutes. Transfer the guinea fowl to a board or platter and tent with foil. Allow to rest for 10 to 15 minutes before cutting.

While the guinea fowl cooks, make the charred tomatoes: Rinse and dry the tomatoes and place them in a grilling basket or cast-iron skillet. Drizzle the tomatoes with the olive oil, sprinkle with the salt and pepper, and place the thyme sprigs over the tomatoes. Roast the tomatoes between the direct and indirect heat on the grill, shaking to ensure even cooking, until they start to blister, 20 to 25 minutes. Taste for seasoning, then discard the thyme.

Make the pickled onion: In a medium nonreactive container, combine the sliced onion and hot pickling liquid and toss to coat. Let sit in the refrigerator for 20 minutes, then remove the onion and drain on a paper towel.

Carefully carve the guinea fowl around the joints and serve with the charred tomatoes, garnished with the onions.

Note: "Spatchcock" is a fancy word for removing the backbone from a piece of poultry. Your butcher may do this, or you can do it yourself by using a pair of kitchen shears to cut out the backbone of the guinea fowl. And don't throw that bone away: you can use it to make your own homemade stock.

THE EAST END WINGS
Crispy Baked Wings with Berbere Honey Glaze and Fried Garlic

Serves 4 to 6

East End Bistro opened in Accra in 2020 with the mission to showcase African cuisine from across all regions. When I was tasked to create the menu for the restaurant, owners Kofi Maafe and Keith Edem wanted a signature dish that was both craveable and handheld. After some trial and error and trying out famous African spice blends, we landed on East African berbere to carry the flavor for an umami-forward wings dish. Berbere is a spicy chili blend that has floral and sweet notes from coriander and cardamom, and when it's paired with a honey glaze, it sets these wings apart from anything else you've ever had. They're perfect to serve as an appetizer or as part of a platter of snacks for a large group.

Chicken Wings

- 2 pounds chicken wings, separated into flats and drumettes
- 1 cup ginger garlic puree, homemade (page 35) or store-bought
- 1½ tablespoons All-Day Seasoning Blend (page 35)
- 1 tablespoon kosher salt
- 2 teaspoons ground coriander
- 2 teaspoons baking powder

Fried Garlic

- 15 garlic cloves
- 2 tablespoons neutral oil

Berbere Honey Glaze

- ¾ cup honey
- 2 tablespoons apple cider vinegar or white wine vinegar
- 2 tablespoons berbere spice blend
- Chopped fresh chives, for garnish

Make the chicken wings: In a large bowl, rub the wings all over with the ginger garlic puree and allow them to marinate in the refrigerator, covered, for at least 4 hours or preferably overnight.

When ready to cook, preheat the oven to 450°F. Line a rimmed baking sheet with foil. Remove the wings from the refrigerator and allow them to come to room temperature. Line a plate with paper towels.

In a small bowl, stir together the seasoning blend, salt, coriander, and baking powder. Sprinkle the mixture over the wings and toss well to coat. Arrange the wings, fatty-side down, on the prepared baking sheet. Bake for 30 minutes, then turn the wings over and bake until golden brown and crispy, 15 to 20 minutes more. Remove the baking sheet from the oven. Drain the wings on the paper towels and allow to cool for 5 minutes.

Meanwhile, make the fried garlic: Smash each clove of garlic, then peel and mince. Line a plate with paper towels and put a fine-mesh sieve over a small heatproof bowl.

Recipe continues

In a small skillet, combine the oil and garlic. Turn the heat to medium and cook until the garlic is lightly golden, 5 to 7 minutes. Remove the skillet from the heat and continue to cook until the garlic is completely golden, 1 more minute. Be careful not to burn the garlic; it will turn bitter if you do. Strain through the sieve; transfer the garlic to the paper towels to cool. (Reserve the garlic oil for another use.)

Make the berbere honey glaze: In a small pot over medium-low heat, warm the honey and vinegar until the honey is looser and less viscous, 5 to 7 minutes. Whisk in the berbere, reduce the heat to low, and cook until the spices are evenly distributed and heated through, about 2 minutes.

In a large bowl, toss the wings with the glaze and fried garlic. Transfer to a platter and serve garnished with chives.

STEWED TURKEY WINGS

Serves 4

Tender turkey wings over white rice reminds me of my childhood. Sitting down at the dinner table, I'd see steam coming off the main dish and a big bowl of white rice on the side, ready to go underneath the wings and soak up their gravy. It was one of those meals that everyone in the house came to sit down at the table for, no matter what else was happening. This recipe is inspired by my mom's eldest sister, my aunty Agatha, who would make stewed turkey wings in a spicy red gravy for us about twice a month. A little bit of time goes a long way in allowing the ginger, tomatoes, and herbs to meld together, so don't rush the cooking process.

Marinade

- 3 pounds turkey wings, cut 1½ inches thick (see Note, page 213)
- 3 tablespoons green seasoning, homemade (page 36) or store-bought
- 2 tablespoons All-Day Seasoning Blend (page 35)
- 2 Scotch bonnet or habanero peppers, stemmed and chopped
- Juice of ½ lime
- 2 teaspoons kosher salt
- 1 teaspoon freshly ground black pepper
- ½ teaspoon ground turmeric
- 1 bunch of thyme

Stew

- 2 tablespoons neutral oil
- 2 tablespoons raw brown sugar or turbinado sugar
- ⅓ cup high-quality extra-virgin olive oil
- ¼ cup tomato paste
- ¼ cup ketchup
- ¼ cup ginger garlic puree, homemade (page 35) or store-bought
- 2 teaspoons Mom's Hot Pepper Sauce (page 45), or store-bought Scotch bonnet hot sauce
- 1½ medium yellow onions, halved and thinly sliced
- 1 red bell pepper, stemmed, seeded, and thinly sliced
- 1 orange bell pepper, stemmed, seeded, and thinly sliced
- 5 garlic cloves, thinly sliced
- 1 (14.5-ounce) can chopped tomatoes
- 2 cups reduced-sodium chicken stock

To Serve

- Cooked white rice, for serving
- ¼ cup (loosely packed) fresh flat-leaf parsley leaves, chopped, for garnish
- Lime wedges, for serving (optional)

Marinate the turkey wings: In a large bowl, season the turkey wings with the green seasoning, seasoning blend, Scotch bonnet peppers, lime juice, salt, black pepper, and turmeric, then add the thyme and mix well. Cover and allow to marinate in the refrigerator for at least 2 hours or up to overnight.

Preheat the oven to 375°F.

Make the stew: In a large, wide, heavy-bottomed ovenproof pot over medium-high heat, add the neutral oil and heat until it begins to shimmer, 2 to 3 minutes. Add the brown sugar and cook, using a wooden spoon to stir frequently, until the sugar caramelizes and becomes loose and looks broken in the oil, 2 to 3 minutes. Reduce the heat to medium. Add the seasoned turkey to the pot without stirring and place a lid over it to stew/steam (a little steam escaping is okay), until the turkey has browned a bit on the bottom, about 5 minutes. Remove the lid and stir the turkey in its juices and brown sugar until all of the pieces are well coated and browned. Place the lid back on and continue to stew for 5 additional minutes, stirring halfway through. Uncover and let cook until the liquid has reduced by half, about 15 minutes. Remove everything from the pot and transfer to a plate.

In the same pot, over medium heat, add the olive oil, tomato paste, ketchup, ginger garlic puree, and hot pepper sauce. Cook, stirring frequently, until the tomato paste takes on a sweet aroma and has tinged the olive oil a red/bronze color, about 3 minutes. Add the onions and red and orange bell peppers and stir to coat with the tomato paste and oil. Cook until softened, stirring occasionally, about 5 minutes. Add the garlic and cook for an additional minute, until fragrant. Carefully add the canned tomatoes and any juices that have collected from the browned turkey and cook, stirring often, until the peppers and onions have collapsed and reduced in size by half, an additional 2 to 3 minutes.

Return the turkey wings to the pot. Add the chicken stock and stir. Move the pot to the oven and bake, uncovered, basting the wings every 20 minutes with the stew, for about 1 hour. Test doneness by piercing the turkey wings with a fork: if the meat comes off the bone easily, they are done. If they're not tender, continue cooking for another 30 minutes and check again. Once the turkey wings are done, remove the pot from the oven and allow to cool for 15 minutes.

Serve over rice, garnished with parsley, and with lime wedges on the side, if you like.

Note: Ask your butcher to cut the wings like oxtail, with a crosscut that will create a more tender dish, or check your frozen meat section near the turkeys for horizontally cut wings. Otherwise, cook them whole and stew them a bit longer.

SHITO FRIED CHICKEN

Serves 4

Fried chicken in Ghana is crispy and packed with a ton of flavor and usually served with a hot pepper sauce. My goal for this recipe is to marry that experience with another way I love to enjoy fried chicken: brined in tangy buttermilk, a style you'd normally see in the American South. Kpakoshito, the spicy and herbaceous green condiment, is used here to impart flavor in combination with buttermilk, which helps carry those flavors and tenderize the bird. Keep this fried chicken recipe in your back pocket to make for a crowd and blow them away, especially with the addition of the smoky, spicy, and sweet berbere honey glaze. It's perfect alone, or used in a fried chicken sandwich if you use boneless chicken pieces.

Brine

2 cups buttermilk

½ cup Kpakoshito Sauce (page 40)

3 large sprigs of thyme

4 large garlic cloves, smashed

2 fresh bay leaves

1 tablespoon kosher salt

1 (4-pound) whole chicken, cut into 8 pieces

Peanut oil, for frying

Dredge

1 cup all-purpose flour

1 cup cornstarch

3 tablespoons All-Day Seasoning Blend (page 35)

1 tablespoon kosher salt

1 cup Berbere Honey Glaze (page 209), warmed, for serving (optional)

Prepare the brine: In a large bowl, combine the buttermilk, kpakoshito, thyme, garlic, bay leaves, and salt. Add the chicken parts and ensure they're submerged in the brine. Cover with plastic wrap and let marinate in the refrigerator for 24 hours.

When ready to cook, place a wire rack over a rimmed baking sheet. Remove the chicken parts from the marinade, arrange them on the rack, and let the excess brine drip off while the chicken comes to room temperature for 30 minutes.

Fill a large heavy-bottomed pot with 3 inches of oil and heat over medium-high heat until the oil reaches 375°F.

Prepare the dredge: In a large bowl, combine the flour, cornstarch, seasoning blend, and salt and whisk to incorporate. Line a plate with paper towels.

Working in batches of 3 or 4 pieces, toss the chicken in the dredge. Ensure all parts of the chicken pieces are well coated in the mixture.

Gently add the coated chicken pieces to the oil. Fry the chicken, being sure to turn the pieces over about halfway through, until the internal temperature reaches 165°F and the crust has a rich, golden brown color, 13 to 15 minutes for larger pieces like breasts and thighs and 8 to 10 minutes for smaller pieces like wings and drumsticks. Transfer the chicken pieces to the paper towels to drain. Repeat the frying process with the remaining chicken.

The tough part: Fit a baking sheet with a wire rack. Arrange the fried chicken pieces on the rack and let them sit for 10 minutes to allow the meat to rest—it's really hot right out of the oil and could burn you if you eat it too soon.

After patiently waiting, serve the chicken, drizzled with warmed berbere honey glaze, if desired.

STICKY TAMARIND-GLAZED DUCK LEGS

Serves 4

Duck confit is a classic French preparation. To confit, or to submerge in fat, is a preservation technique that requires your duck to be slowly cooked in its own fat, resulting in meat with an almost silky texture. But my version is flavored with a marinade and sauce that are affectionately West African and Caribbean. Before the duck is confited, a cure is used to penetrate the duck with intense seasoning from salt, aromatics, and herbs—enter green seasoning. Caribbean green seasoning is a powerhouse of blended herbs and aromatics that acts as the base for so many dishes from the islands, from vinaigrettes to curry goat. The dish is finished with a tamarind glaze that is the perfect lacquer for the duck. It's tangy and sweet, and has a warming heat and bit of funk. You'll know the time used to make this dish is well worth it when you take that first bite.

4 duck legs (about 2 pounds total)

1 tablespoon plus 1 teaspoon kosher salt

½ cup plus 2 tablespoons green seasoning, homemade (page 36) or store-bought

15 sprigs of thyme

1 tablespoon whole black peppercorns

3 to 4 cups rendered duck fat, as needed

¾ cup Tamarind Glaze (recipe follows)

Fried Peanut Salsa (page 186), for serving

Silky Yam Puree (page 146), for serving

Season the duck legs all over with the salt. In a nonreactive baking dish that can fit the duck legs in a single layer, spread half the green seasoning in an even layer and scatter half the thyme sprigs and peppercorns over. Arrange the duck legs skin-side up in a single layer on top, pressing the legs into the green seasoning. Place the remaining thyme sprigs and peppercorns over the duck legs, then add the remaining green seasoning, making sure the legs are completely coated. Cover tightly with plastic wrap and refrigerate for 24 to 48 hours.

When ready to cook, preheat the oven to 225°F. Remove the duck legs from the refrigerator and allow to come to room temperature.

In a small pot over medium-low heat, heat the duck fat until melted but barely warm.

Remove the duck legs from the green seasoning cure. Wipe away as much of the cure as you can and rinse under cold water to remove all of the seasoning. Pat the duck legs dry with paper towels, then arrange them in a single layer in a large baking dish. Pour the duck fat over the legs, making sure the legs are completely submerged.

Cover the baking dish with a lid or foil and cook the duck until it is completely tender and the skin pulls away from the drumstick, about 3½ hours.

If serving later, remove the duck from the oven and let cool completely at room temperature while in the baking dish, submerged in fat. Once completely cooled, cover

Recipe continues

tightly with plastic wrap or the lid and transfer to the refrigerator to cool. The duck will keep in an airtight container in the refrigerator for up to 3 weeks. An hour or so before serving, remove the duck from the refrigerator and allow it to come to room temperature before searing.

If serving immediately, heat a large skillet over medium heat. Carefully remove the duck legs from the fat, wiping away any excess. Place the legs in the skillet and sear until golden brown all over, about 5 minutes per side, then remove from the heat. Brush the legs with the tamarind glaze. Serve immediately with the yam puree, topped with the peanut salsa.

Tamarind Glaze
Makes 1½ cups

Tamarind, a native African ingredient, is just as versatile as it is delicious. For years I knew tamarind only as an ingredient used in drinks and teas. It wasn't until I moved to Washington, D.C., in 2016 that I was introduced to two different versions of a savory-sweet tamarind glaze while working at Kingbird and Kith/Kin restaurants with chefs Mike Santoro and Kwame Onwuachi. Inspired by both restaurants, I combined the two glazes into this recipe that doubles down on the savory-sweet and umami.

2 tablespoons high-quality extra-virgin olive oil

¼ cup golden raisins

½ medium shallot, minced

2 garlic cloves, minced

1 (1-inch) piece of fresh ginger, peeled and minced

1 cup coarsely chopped palm sugar from a block

½ cup seedless tamarind paste

⅓ cup honey

2 tablespoons fish sauce

1 tablespoon fresh lime juice, plus more to taste

Kosher salt

1 small bunch of chives, thinly sliced

In a medium pot over medium-high heat, add the olive oil, raisins, shallot, garlic, and ginger and sweat, stirring frequently, until fragrant, 2 to 3 minutes. Raise the heat to high, add ¾ cup of water, and bring to a boil. Add the palm sugar and tamarind paste and reduce the heat to medium-low so the mixture simmers. Cook, whisking constantly, until the mixture looks like shiny paste, 10 to 15 minutes. Remove the pot from the heat and allow to cool slightly.

Add the mixture to a blender and blend into a smooth paste. Pass the mixture through a fine-mesh sieve into a small bowl. Return the strained mixture to the pot and place over low heat. Stir in the honey, fish sauce, and lime juice. Cook until the mixture reduces to the consistency of warm caramel, about 3 minutes. Let cool for at least 10 minutes. Taste and season with salt and additional lime juice, if desired. Fold in the chives. The glaze will keep in an airtight container in the refrigerator for 2 weeks.

OXTAIL STEW

Serves 4 to 6

"There's only one oxtail per ox!" When I was a kid, that was the endearing warning whenever the oxtail stew served by the Caribbean restaurant near my church in the Bronx was running low. This recipe speaks to those memories, taking me back to the Sundays of my childhood. Oxtails come from the steer's tail, which, as you can imagine, is a well-exercised muscle that ironically also has a high fat content and marbling throughout the meat. This dish is slow-and-low cooking at its best. Deep flavors from fresh thyme, allspice, Scotch bonnet, and a plethora of other ingredients intensify as the oxtails braise into a fatty, gelatinous, chewy deliciousness. In West Africa, oxtails are typically served with yams or white rice. In the Caribbean, peas and rice are more of what you would normally see with this dish.

Marinade

2½ pounds oxtails

¼ cup (packed) dark brown sugar

3 tablespoons green seasoning, homemade (page 36) or store-bought

2 tablespoons soy sauce

2 tablespoons Worcestershire sauce

2 tablespoons All-Day Seasoning Blend (page 35)

2 teaspoons ground allspice

2 teaspoons browning sauce

1 tablespoon kosher salt

Stew

2 tablespoons neutral oil

2½ cups beef stock, plus more as needed

1 tablespoon chopped or crumbled palm sugar from a block

1 large yellow onion, cut into medium dice

1 large red bell pepper, stemmed, seeded, and cut into medium dice

4 scallions, coarsely chopped plus more for garnish (white and green parts)

2 small carrots, diced

2 tablespoons minced garlic

1 (1-inch) piece of fresh ginger, peeled and thinly sliced

1 Scotch bonnet or habanero pepper, stemmed, seeded, and diced

1 heaping tablespoon tomato paste

6 to 8 allspice berries

1 tablespoon fresh thyme leaves

1 tablespoon ketchup

2 fresh bay leaves

1 (15-ounce) can butter beans, rinsed and drained

1 tablespoon cornstarch

Peas and Rice (page 168) or cooked white rice, for serving

Marinate the oxtails: Clean the oxtails by removing any hanging fat and sinew. In a large bowl, mix the brown sugar, green seasoning, soy sauce, Worcestershire sauce, seasoning blend, ground allspice, browning sauce, and salt. Add the oxtails to the bowl and rub the seasoning mixture into them. Cover the bowl and transfer to the refrigerator to marinate for at least 4 hours or preferably overnight.

When you're ready to cook, transfer the oxtails to a plate and set aside at room temperature. Reserve the marinade.

Make the stew: Heat the oil in a large Dutch oven over medium-high heat. When the oil is hot, sear the oxtails on all sides until browned, 3 to 5 minutes per side (you may need to work in batches to avoid overcrowding the pan). Raise or reduce the heat as needed to keep the meat from burning. Transfer the seared oxtails to a plate. Repeat with the remaining oxtails and set aside.

Recipe continues

Deglaze the Dutch oven by adding 2 tablespoons of the beef stock and scraping the browned bits from the bottom of the pot. Over medium-high heat, add the palm sugar to the pot and cook, stirring frequently, until it starts to dissolve, about 30 seconds. Add the onion and cook, stirring often, until translucent, about 3 minutes. Add the bell pepper, scallions, carrots, garlic, ginger, and Scotch bonnet pepper. Cook, stirring often, until the onion has softened, about 5 minutes. Stir in the tomato paste and allspice berries and cook, stirring frequently, until the paste browns slightly, 2 to 3 minutes.

Add the oxtails back to the pot. Stir in the reserved oxtail marinade, remaining beef broth, the thyme, ketchup, and bay leaves. The beef stock should cover most of your oxtails; add more stock if necessary. Bring the mixture to a boil, then reduce the heat to low and cover the pot with the lid slightly cracked.

Braise the oxtails, undisturbed, until the meat starts to fall away from the bone, 2 to 2½ hours.

Remove the lid and stir in the butter beans and continue to simmer, uncovered, to meld the flavors, another 20 minutes. Remove the bay leaves. In a small bowl, make a slurry by whisking the cornstarch with 1½ tablespoons of water. Stir the slurry into the pot and raise the heat to medium, stirring until the mixture thickens.

Serve hot over peas and rice or white rice. Garnish with diced scallion.

Note: This dish can be made in a pressure cooker. Follow the recipe up until the oxtails begin to braise, then follow the manufacturer's instructions to pressure cook for 45 minutes to 1 hour.

BENNE MISO NOODLES
with Ground Beef

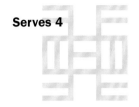

Serves 4

When I was a broke culinary school student, I became very familiar with instant noodles, learning how to doctor them up to make them taste the best. I later learned that Indomie and other popular brands of instant noodles are enjoyed in many countries, including those in West Africa, where they're an affordable meal option for so many. These days, it isn't uncommon to see noodle dishes on restaurant menus throughout Accra. This recipe was inspired by a delicious noodle dish I had at a restaurant in Osu called Kōzo that was a perfect blend of East Asian and African flavors.

3 teaspoons kosher salt

5 scallions, coarsely chopped (white and green parts)

3 garlic cloves

1 Fresno chili, halved and seeded

1 (thumb-size) piece of fresh ginger, peeled

1 bunch broccolini, ends trimmed

1 pound dried ramen noodles

2 teaspoons toasted sesame oil

6 tablespoons avocado oil

1 pound ground beef (80/20)

2 tablespoons All-Day Seasoning Blend (page 35)

2 tablespoons benne miso (for sourcing, see page 25)

2 teaspoons dark soy sauce

1 tablespoon chopped palm sugar from a block, or turbinado sugar

1 cup enoki or seafood mushrooms, root ends trimmed

2 teaspoons white benne seeds (for sourcing, see page 25) or sesame seeds, toasted

Bring a large pot of water to a boil over high heat and add 2 teaspoons of the kosher salt. Meanwhile, finely dice the scallions, garlic, chili, and ginger, and chop the broccolini into smaller pieces, about 1 inch long. Add the noodles to the boiling water and cook for half of the time recommended on the package. Reserve ¼ cup of the cooking water, then drain the noodles, toss with the sesame oil, and set aside.

In a large nonstick pan, heat 3 tablespoons of the avocado oil over medium heat until it shimmers. Line a plate with paper towels. Add the ground beef, seasoning blend, and remaining 1 teaspoon of salt to the pan. Cook, stirring often to break up the ground beef, until the beef is thoroughly browned, about 5 minutes. Transfer the beef to the paper towels. Using another paper towel, wipe away any fat that remains in the pan and set the pan aside.

In a small bowl, dissolve the benne miso in the reserved cooking water. Add the soy sauce and stir to combine.

In the same nonstick pan that you cooked the beef in, add the remaining 3 tablespoons of avocado oil and heat over medium heat until shimmering. Add the palm sugar. Cook, stirring, until the sugar dissolves, about 10 seconds. Add all of the garlic, chili, and ginger and half of the scallions. Sauté, stirring frequently, until fragrant and slightly toasted, about 30 seconds. Add the broccolini and sauté until the greens have cooked down and all the liquid has evaporated, an additional 3 minutes.

Add the parcooked noodles, mushrooms, cooked ground beef, and miso–soy sauce mixture and sauté, stirring frequently, until the noodles are evenly coated with sauce and hot, about 3 minutes.

Divide the noodles among 4 plates and sprinkle with the toasted white benne seeds and the remaining scallions. Serve immediately.

CHICHINGA

Serves 6 to 8

These are the quintessential Ghanaian kebabs, but really they belong to most West African homes. Chichinga is often one of the many rounds of food you receive during a welcome at someone's home or at an event in the Ghanaian community. My take uses my All-Day Seasoning Blend and Suya Spice Blend to season the meat, but this is very similar to what you might have at any gathering. And if chichinga is served in a restaurant or on a roadside in Ghana, you'll get it the way it's meant to be enjoyed: over the grill. Suya spices just seem to come alive when cooked over a flame; that's why I think this dish stands on its own against any other version of kebabs in the world.

2 pounds sirloin steak

3 tablespoons ginger garlic puree, homemade (page 35) or store-bought

2 tablespoons All-Day Seasoning Blend (page 35)

1½ tablespoons kosher salt

2 teaspoons tomato paste

1 teaspoon sweet paprika

¾ cup Suya Spice Blend (page 35), plus more for garnish

⅓ cup neutral oil

2 medium red onions, cut into large dice (½ inch)

2 red bell peppers, stemmed, seeded, and cut into large dice (½ inch)

2 yellow bell peppers, stemmed, seeded, and cut into large dice (½ inch)

Sea salt, for garnish

Special Equipment

8 to 10 metal or wooden skewers (if using wooden skewers, soak overnight in water)

Place the steak on a cutting board and cover with a layer of plastic wrap. Using a meat tenderizer (or a rolling pin), pound the meat to a ¼-inch thickness. Cut the steak into 1-inch squares and transfer to a large bowl. In a small bowl, combine the ginger garlic puree, seasoning blend, salt, tomato paste, paprika, and half of the suya and mix well to combine. Drizzle the mixture over the steak and toss, being sure to coat all pieces of steak in the suya mixture. Set aside.

In a small bowl, stir together the remaining suya and the oil.

Arrange the onions, red and yellow bell peppers, and sirloin on skewers, alternating ingredients and with about 3 pieces of sirloin per skewer. Place the kebabs on a baking sheet. Brush half the suya oil mixture over the kebabs, then transfer to the refrigerator to marinate for 1 hour. When ready to cook, remove the kebabs from the refrigerator and allow to come to room temperature.

While the kebabs are coming to temperature, preheat an outdoor grill to high heat (about 550°F).

Place the kebabs on the heated grates and grill, turning frequently using tongs or a grill glove and basting with the remaining suya oil mixture, until the vegetables and meat are slightly charred and the vegetables are tender, 5 to 8 minutes total.

To serve, transfer the kebabs to a platter and sprinkle with additional suya and sea salt.

YASSA LAMB BURGERS

Serves 4

Yassa poulet, the national dish of Senegal made of caramelized onions and chicken flavored with a bit of Dijon mustard and lemon juice, is such a luscious dish. It's also one that speaks to the ingenuity of African cooks to combine ingredients from somewhere else (in this case, France) with the time-honored tradition of stews and sauces that have had ample opportunity to meld into one beautiful meal. I wanted to make a burger highlighting the jam-like consistency that onions take on in yassa poulet, so I took the whole concept, stripped it down, and turned it into a condiment similar to chutney. I love this recipe so much because it reminds me of Senegalese chef Pierre Thiam, the cooking practices of Ghana, and my favorite aspects of some of the best burgers I've had over the course of my travels. Usually with a burger, the meat is the star of the show, but here the yassa jam steals the spotlight: it's savory and tart. I always encourage people to add whatever they want to their burgers, so create a spread of toppings along with the aioli, tomatoes, mixed fresh greens or lettuce, and the warmed yassa onions.

Yassa Onion Jam

- 4 tablespoons (½ stick) unsalted butter
- 2 medium white onions, thinly sliced
- 3 tablespoons white balsamic vinegar or champagne vinegar
- 2 tablespoons Roasted Garlic Puree (page 36)
- 1 tablespoon ground turmeric
- 2 teaspoons Dijon mustard
- ½ teaspoon ground coriander
- 1 to 2 tablespoons fresh lemon juice, to taste
- 1 teaspoon kosher salt, or more to taste

Aioli

- ¾ cup mayonnaise
- 2 tablespoons Roasted Garlic Puree (page 36)
- 1 tablespoon fresh lemon juice
- 1 teaspoon kosher salt

Burgers

- 1 pound ground lamb (see Note, page 232)
- 3 sprigs of thyme, leaves removed and chopped
- 1 sprig of rosemary, leaves removed and chopped
- 1 tablespoon garlic powder

- 1 tablespoon kosher salt
- 1 tablespoon freshly ground black pepper

To Serve

- 4 hamburger buns, bulkie rolls, or potato rolls, split
- Lettuce leaves
- Thinly sliced tomato

Make the yassa onion jam: In a medium saucepan, melt 2 tablespoons of the butter over medium-high heat. Add the onions and cook, stirring frequently, until they are soft and golden brown, about 18 minutes.

Add the vinegar, roasted garlic puree, turmeric, Dijon, and coriander. Reduce the heat to low and cook, stirring occasionally, until the mixture is well combined and becomes a mahogany color, 5 to 7 minutes. Remove from the heat, then stir in the remaining 2 tablespoons of butter, the lemon juice, and salt. Taste and add more salt, if desired. Set aside and keep warm. (The jam can be made a day or two in advance and warmed before serving.)

Recipe continues

Make the aioli: In a small bowl, mix the mayonnaise, roasted garlic puree, lemon juice, and salt. Set aside.

Preheat the oven to 350°F (for toasting the buns; they can also be warmed in a skillet with a little butter).

Make the burgers: In a medium bowl, thoroughly mix together the lamb, thyme, rosemary, garlic powder, salt, and pepper; shape into 4 balls.

Heat a cast-iron skillet or grill pan over medium-high heat until very hot and smoking. Working in batches as necessary to avoid crowding, add 2 meat balls to the pan at a time. Use a spatula to smash them into patties 4 inches across and ¼ inch thick. Cook until the edges of the patties start to crisp up, about 4 minutes, then use the spatula to carefully flip the patties. Cook until hot and slightly pink in the center, another 5 minutes, or until they reach your desired degree of doneness. Transfer the burgers to a plate, cover them loosely with foil, and cook the remaining burgers.

Get ready to serve: While the burgers are cooking, arrange the opened hamburger buns on a baking sheet and toast in the oven until golden brown, about 2 minutes.

Coat the top buns with heaping tablespoons of aioli, then coat the bottom buns with the same amount. Top each bottom bun with a lettuce leaf, a lamb patty, ¼ cup of the yassa onions, tomato slices, and then the top bun. Alternatively, lay out all components and allow guests to assemble their burgers themselves. Serve immediately.

Note: This recipe works great with ground beef too.

LABADI PORK RIBS

Serves 3 to 4

Labadi Beach on the coast of Accra faces the Atlantic Ocean, and often people build fires and hang out there late at night. During a recent trip, I saw a woman near the beach making a sauce with sorghum syrup, garlic, crushed red pepper flakes, and a bit of tamarind that she then brushed frequently on a grilled bird over charcoals. The sauce was spicy, sweet, and full of flavor and stayed with me long afterward. From that memory, I developed my own version for ribs, and I started teaching it in my virtual cooking classes. It's so good: tacky and sticky and like meat candy. This is one of the most requested dishes I make, and even better, it's low maintenance, making it a perfect easy dinner dish with rice and a salad or grilled vegetables.

1 (2½-pound) rack pork ribs

3 tablespoons (packed) light brown sugar

2 teaspoons kosher salt

½ teaspoon freshly ground black pepper

1 cup Labadi Sauce (recipe follows), plus more for serving

Line a rimmed baking sheet with foil. Clean the ribs of any silver skin or membrane on the bone side. Pat dry with paper towels, then place on the prepared baking sheet. In a small bowl, mix the brown sugar, salt, and pepper, then rub the mixture all over the ribs. Place the ribs in the refrigerator, uncovered, for at least 4 hours or up to overnight.

When ready to cook, preheat the oven to 300°F.

Wrap the ribs tightly with foil and place on a baking sheet. Bake until tender and beginning to fall off the bone, about 3 hours. Let the ribs rest and cool to room temperature while still wrapped in foil (they can be transferred to the refrigerator for up to 5 days at this point if you're prepping ahead).

Preheat the broiler to medium-high heat. In a small saucepan, warm the Labadi sauce.

Unwrap the ribs and put them on a rimmed baking sheet. Using a brush or the back of a spoon, glaze the ribs all over with the sauce. Finish the ribs by broiling them until the glaze bubbles, 3 to 5 minutes. Remove from the heat, cut the ribs into smaller portions, and serve alongside more Labadi sauce.

Recipe continues

Labadi Sauce
Makes 1⅔ cups

As a chef, one of the fun parts about my job is re-creating flavors from my memories. To this day, I can remember that vendor in Accra and how she basted her grilled meats with a tamarind-based sauce that tasted like A1 Sauce with more depth and sweetness. When I got back to the States, I went into my kitchen and experimented until I came up with a similar sauce. Balanced and super delicious, it's acidic with some funk and some sweetness and makes a great marinade for grilled chicken breasts as well.

3 tablespoons crushed red pepper flakes

½ cup avocado oil

¼ cup minced garlic

¼ cup sorghum syrup

¼ cup agave syrup

¼ cup cane vinegar or apple cider vinegar

¼ cup fish sauce

¼ cup tamarind concentrate (I like Tamicon)

¼ cup (packed) dark brown sugar

Place the red pepper flakes in a small heat-resistant bowl and set a fine-mesh sieve over the bowl. In a small pot, heat the oil over medium heat. When the oil is hot, add the garlic and fry until it turns evenly golden, 3 to 4 minutes; watch carefully and stir often to keep from burning the garlic. Strain the garlic oil onto the red pepper flakes. Reserve the fried garlic and the chili oil.

In the same pot, combine the sorghum syrup, agave syrup, cane vinegar, fish sauce, tamarind concentrate, and brown sugar and bring to a boil. Set the fine-mesh sieve over a liquid measuring cup and strain the chili oil through it. Add all the red pepper flakes and ¼ cup of the oil (reserve the remaining oil for another use) to the pot and cook, stirring constantly to keep the glaze from burning or bubbling over, until it coats the back of a spoon, 7 to 10 minutes. Don't worry if the glaze doesn't seem emulsified—it will come together easily (and continue to thicken) once it cools. Stir in the fried garlic.

Labadi sauce will keep in an airtight container in the refrigerator for up to 7 days.

DESSERTS

We Carry the Past and the Future Within Ourselves

*It'd be remiss of me not to acknowledge the present moment in cooking and Ameri-*can culture in this cookbook. Conversations about Africa and its influence have been happening for a long time, but now it feels as if the world is finally looking toward the continent for inspiration and to understand how deeply tied we all are to it. As I've been teaching people in their homes how to cook and getting to connect with them over these last few years, it's all made me think about my work more deeply. How can I make sure I'm progressing and helping the next generation of chefs who look like me? How can I be sure I'm sharing my unique perspective while also tapping into what connects us all?

When I pull back and think about this moment in food culture and the world at large, it strikes me as a very pivotal point in time. The world has gotten smaller in some ways: I can see what people are doing on the other side of the world via a device that fits in the palm of my hand. I can virtually venture into different cuisines through photos, learn about different spices and plants online, and talk to chefs from across the world. I can order ingredients from anywhere to be shipped to my home without ever getting up from the couch. It feels like a blessing. Being able to connect with chefs from all over the world, who take their craft seriously and want to push it forward while preserving traditions, is such a great experience. We share ideas, successes, and failures with one another, and I really believe that this comradery is the tide that raises all ships. I see myself and them as ambassadors of the continent, bringing people into the cuisine but also speaking to our shared history.

That history and the stories of my ancestors from Ghana, of other ancestors from the continent, and of the ones who were forced to endure the journey across the Atlantic are so integral to the foodways of the New World. To me, dishes like fufu, waakye, and stewed turkey are more than just a meal because there's a history and education that come along with eating, and that's why storytelling is so important. Descendants of that history, both on the continent and in other regions of the world, have not had the opportunity to tell that story from their unique point of view. I want that element of storytelling to stay a part of this cuisine and a part of the movement of these chefs because people need to know that these dishes are part of a global fabric—and a big part of American foodways.

The biggest duality I face now is tailoring the way I cook to different markets while not bending or compromising to other people's palates. I try to keep in mind how people eat in different parts of the world and be sensitive to that, while keeping in mind what my tastes are. As a chef, you should be open and meet diners where they are, but I also have a duty to stay true to myself and what I like to create and eat. In Ghana, I punch up my recipes with more spice and heat, and understand that the concepts of medium-rare and raw preparations of food don't really exist. So there I focus on using traditional ingredients in a surprising way. For a dinner in Jamaica, I served a goat stew made with green seasoning alongside a jollof risotto, highlighting a key dish of West Africa but in a way that people may not have seen before, showing that West African flavors are versatile and dynamic.

I'll always feel the push-pull of modernity and tradition, but that's where I want to be because it keeps me searching, keeps pushing me to be a better cook. I feel like I have a bit more freedom to play around with ingredients and techniques. That might sound challenging or hard, but I would say it's just me.

My hope, as time moves forward, is that other chefs can continue to evolve creatively as well, pushing the parameters of what African cooking is and what the public thinks of when they hear about a Black or African chef. That means stepping outside of your comfort zone and allowing your culture and surroundings to influence the food you cook. I want people to be inspired the same way I've been inspired by my travels, by taking a deeper look at the connections between Ghana and America. It feels like by the end of the next decade, things are going to be different in my world, and the food world at large. I'm hopeful there will be more stories and more storytellers on all sides of the diaspora sharing their unique perspectives about food and culture. I hope they tell the history of dishes while also showing how things have evolved over time, and discuss the ingenuity of our ancestors to create these dishes that we're still exploring centuries later.

BOFROT
Puff–Puff

Makes about 20

Bofrot have always been a part of my life. They're a great holiday dish and a real crowd-pleaser. At any Ghanaian celebration or get-together, you'll see aunties making bofrot, fishing the sweet, golden brown balls out of a large pot of fryer oil and then letting them drain on paper towels before they're devoured by both children and adults. I make them often at home, coating the freshly fried balls in cinnamon and sugar before giving them to my daughter. Bofrot are one of her favorite things to eat too, and she enjoys them as much as I did as a kid.

1½ cups (360g) lukewarm whole milk (110°F)

4 teaspoons active dry yeast

⅔ cup (135g) sugar

3 cups (360g) sifted all-purpose flour

1½ teaspoons kosher salt

½ teaspoon freshly grated calabash nutmeg (for sourcing, see page 25) or nutmeg

4 cups (950g) neutral oil, for frying

Spiced Sugar (Optional)

¼ cup (50g) sugar

½ tablespoon ground cinnamon

½ teaspoon freshly grated calabash nutmeg (for sourcing, see page 25) or nutmeg

Pour the warm milk in a medium bowl, then sprinkle with the yeast and 1 teaspoon of the sugar and stir to combine. Set aside until the yeast begins to foam, 5 to 8 minutes. Meanwhile, in a large bowl, combine the flour, the remaining sugar, the salt, and nutmeg and whisk to combine.

Pour the yeast mixture into the flour mixture and mix with a wooden spoon or your hands until there are no visible lumps of flour, scraping down the sides of the bowl with a rubber spatula as needed, 2 to 3 minutes.

Cover the bowl with a kitchen towel and let the dough rise at room temperature until there are bubbles all over the surface of the dough and it has doubled in bulk, about 2 hours.

In a deep, 10-inch straight-sided skillet over medium heat, heat the oil to 350°F. Fit a baking sheet with a wire rack.

Spray a medium ice cream scoop (you can also use clean hands or a large dinner spoon) with a bit of cooking spray, then scoop the batter in 1-tablespoon portions into the oil, making sure not to overcrowd the pan so that the oil temperature stays consistent (fry about 6 per batch). Fry, flipping occasionally, until golden brown all over and the dough reaches an internal temperature of 190°F, 4 to 6 minutes total. (See the Note if the bofrot are browning too quickly.) Remove the finished bofrot with a slotted spoon and place on the rack. Repeat with the remaining dough.

If you like, make the spiced sugar: In a small bowl, mix the sugar, cinnamon, and nutmeg until well combined. Toss the warm bofrot in the mixture to coat.

Serve the bofrot warm or at room temperature.

Note: If the bofrot aren't cooked all the way through after frying, arrange them on a wire rack set inside a rimmed baking sheet and bake at 350°F until a thermometer inserted into the center reads about 190°F.

BANANA FRITTERS

Serves 4 to 6

When I speak with friends about food from Africa, a popular childhood snack that comes to mind for all of us is banana fritters. They are typically made by mashing ripe bananas, which are ideal for taste and texture, and combining them with flour and spices into a flavorful batter. The fritters are fried until golden with a crispy, airy exterior. I like to dust mine with confectioners' sugar, but they can also be served with honey or melted chocolate if you like.

1½ cups (210g) all-purpose flour

3 tablespoons (packed) light brown sugar

½ teaspoon ground cinnamon

¼ teaspoon ground nutmeg

3 large eggs

1 cup (240g) whole milk

½ teaspoon rum extract (optional)

4 medium ripe bananas

Neutral oil, for frying

¼ cup (30g) confectioners' sugar, for dusting

In a large bowl, sift the flour, brown sugar, cinnamon, and nutmeg together. With a whisk, beat in the eggs one at a time until well incorporated. Whisking constantly, gradually add the milk, about ⅓ cup (80g) at a time, and continue to whisk until the batter is smooth, then add the rum extract (if using).

Peel the bananas, then add them to a separate small bowl. Using a fork, mash the bananas until you have a chunky puree. Stir the puree into the batter and allow the mixture to rest at room temperature for about 30 minutes before frying.

Pour 2 to 3 inches of oil into a deep fryer or large, heavy saucepan. Heat the oil until it reaches 375°F. Line a plate with paper towels.

For each fritter, ladle ¼ cup of the batter into the hot oil. Fry 2 or 3 fritters at a time until the fritters are golden on all sides, about 3 minutes. Transfer the finished fritters to the paper towels to drain. Dust with confectioners' sugar, then serve immediately.

CONDENSED MILK CAKE

Makes one 10-inch cake

Here is my take on a pound cake, a classic, simple dessert that you can serve for any event or holiday. This recipe is flavored with sweetened condensed milk, a staple throughout Africa and the Caribbean that is used for teas, coffee, and baked goods like this one. It can be topped with whatever seasonal fruit is available, like peaches, strawberries, oranges, or cherries.

½ cup (1 stick / 115g) unsalted butter

2 cups (280g) all-purpose flour, plus more for the pan

2 teaspoons baking powder

½ teaspoon ground nutmeg

½ teaspoon kosher salt

¾ cup (150g) sugar

6 tablespoons (90g) cream cheese, at room temperature

1 (14-ounce / 395g) can sweetened condensed milk

1 tablespoon high-quality extra-virgin olive oil

1 teaspoon grated lemon zest

1 tablespoon fresh lemon juice

½ teaspoon almond extract or vanilla extract

4 large eggs, at room temperature

Preheat the oven to 350°F. Use 1 tablespoon of the butter to grease a 10- to 12-cup Bundt pan, being sure to get into all the grooves. Sprinkle with flour and tap out any excess.

In a medium bowl, whisk together the flour, baking powder, nutmeg, and salt.

In a large bowl (if using an electric handheld mixer) or in the bowl of a stand mixer fitted with the paddle attachment, cream the remaining 7 tablespoons (100g) of butter, the sugar, and cream cheese at medium speed until light and fluffy, 3 to 5 minutes. Scrape down the sides of the bowl with a spatula. Add the condensed milk and olive oil and beat on medium-high speed until well combined, about 1 minute, and scrape down the sides of the bowl. Add the lemon zest, lemon juice, and almond extract, and beat on medium speed until well incorporated, 1 minute more. Add the eggs one at a time, beating until thoroughly incorporated between additions and scraping down the sides of the bowl as needed.

Add the dry ingredients to the wet and beat on low speed until just combined, with no streaks of dry ingredients remaining. Scrape into the prepared pan and smooth the surface with the spatula.

Bake until golden brown and a cake tester inserted into the center comes out clean, 50 to 55 minutes. Let the cake cool for 10 minutes in the pan, then turn out onto a wire rack. Let cool completely before slicing into wedges to serve.

The cake can be wrapped tightly in plastic wrap and stored in a cool, dry place for up to 5 days.

MALVA PUDDING

Serves 8 to 16

I'm confident in stating that South African malva pudding is my favorite dessert of all time. Funnily enough, I never had it while in South Africa—my first time was in a restaurant in Harlem called Madiba. A few years later, I saw it again in a Ghanaian patisserie while in Accra. Both experiences of this spongy apricot cake drenched in an otherworldly custard left me speechless. It's a tacky, sweet, and moist cake that can easily be enjoyed on its own but is taken to the next level with a scoop of ice cream. I researched this recipe and eventually added it to East End Bistro's dessert offerings, where it quickly became the most popular dessert on that menu.

¾ cup plus 2 tablespoons (125g) all-purpose flour

2 teaspoons baking powder

½ teaspoon baking soda

¾ cup (150g) sugar

¾ cup (175g) whole milk

2 large eggs

1 teaspoon kosher salt

1 tablespoon unsalted butter, melted

1 tablespoon apricot jam

1 teaspoon apple cider vinegar

Glaze

⅔ cup (160g) heavy cream

⅔ cup (130g) sugar

6 tablespoons (85g) cold unsalted butter, diced

1 teaspoon kosher salt

Position a rack in the center of the oven and preheat the oven to 375°F. Spray an 8-inch square cake pan with nonstick baking spray.

In a small bowl, whisk together the flour, baking powder, and baking soda. Set aside.

In a stand mixer fitted with the whisk attachment, or in a medium bowl if using an electric handheld mixer, beat the sugar, milk, eggs, and salt on medium speed until the mixture is pourable, about 2 minutes. Mix in the melted butter, apricot jam, and vinegar on high speed until well combined, 2 minutes.

Add the flour mixture in thirds and mix on medium speed, scraping down the sides of the bowl as needed, until there are no streaks remaining. The batter should be smooth and lump-free.

Pour the batter into the prepared pan. Bake the cake until it is golden on top and a cake tester inserted into the center comes out clean or with a few moist crumbs, 20 to 30 minutes. Let the cake cool in the pan on a wire rack until slightly warm, about 15 minutes.

While the cake is baking, make the glaze: In a medium pot, combine the cream, sugar, butter, salt, and 3 tablespoons of water. Warm over medium-low heat, whisking gently, until the butter is melted and the mixture is smooth, about 3 minutes. Remove from the heat and cover to keep warm while the cake bakes. (You should have about 1½ cups of glaze.)

After the cake has cooled for about 15 minutes, use a toothpick to poke small holes throughout the cake. Pour all of the glaze evenly over the surface of the cake. Allow the glaze to soak into the cake for 2 minutes, then slice into 8 large squares (or 16 small ones) and serve warm.

The pudding will keep in an airtight container or in squares wrapped in plastic wrap in the refrigerator for 1 week.

NKATE CAKE

Serves 4

This brittle-like sweet holds a special place in the hearts of a lot of West Africans, specifically because for many who grew up in the region, it was a common snack during our school days. It's truly dealer's choice on how fine or coarse you like the peanuts in your brittle, but regardless of your preference, your brittle should be chewy, crunchy, and tacky. If it sticks to the roof of your mouth, you're in business.

1 tablespoon neutral oil, for rolling

1 pound (450g) unsalted raw peanuts

1 cup (225g) castor sugar

½ lemon

1½ teaspoons flaky sea salt

Position a rack in the center of the oven and preheat the oven to 325°F. Pour the oil on a cutting board and rolling pin and rub all over. (This is meant to help prevent the nkate cake from sticking once it has cooled.)

Spread the raw peanuts evenly on a rimmed baking sheet and bake, stirring occasionally, until the peanuts start to release a deep aroma, 10 to 12 minutes. Let cool.

Place the peanuts in a zip-top bag and crush them into smaller pieces (the size is up to you) with the oiled rolling pin. (If you have a food processor, you can use the pulse function for this step.)

In a medium nonstick saucepan, add the sugar, 3 tablespoons of water, and a few drops of lemon juice. Over medium heat, cook the sugar, swirling it around and letting it dissolve, until it reaches 320°F on a candy thermometer and is a light caramel color, about 4½ minutes.

Add the crushed peanuts to the caramel and stir quickly until properly combined. Immediately turn the mixture out onto the oiled board. Spread the mixture with the oiled rolling pin to flatten it to a ⅓-inch-thick rectangle (the other dimensions don't matter!). Be sure to work on the nkate cake quickly while it is hot. Sprinkle the salt on top. Using a sharp knife, cut the rectangle on the diagonal into strips and let it cool completely.

Once cooled, break the nkate cake into pieces. The cake will keep in an airtight container in a cool, dark place for up to 7 days.

MANGO TART
with Rum Marshmallow

Makes one 9- or 10-inch tart

I served this mango tart as the last course for a summer dinner in Bermuda at the Loren at Pink Beach Hotel. Mangos are one of my favorite fruits because of their tart-forward yet still sweet taste. Pairing mango with the flavor of rum brings to mind beaches, islands, and warm weather. This tart is in no way a traditional take on anything but rather a celebration of two ingredients that I enjoy even more in tandem than apart, and that have contributed so much to the economics and cultural identity of people of West Africa, the Caribbean, and Latin America.

Mango Pastry Cream

⅔ cup (120g) sugar

4 large egg yolks

3 tablespoons cornstarch

2½ tablespoons pastry flour

½ teaspoon ground green cardamom

Kosher salt

1½ cups (360g) whole milk

½ cup (100g) fresh, canned, or thawed frozen mango puree or pulp (I like Deep brand canned alphonso mango)

¼ cup plus 3 tablespoons (105g) heavy cream

¼ vanilla bean, split and seeds scraped out and reserved, or ½ teaspoon vanilla extract

2 tablespoons fresh lime juice

2 tablespoons cold unsalted butter, cut into small pieces

Pâte Sucrée

¼ cup plus ½ tablespoon (55g) sugar

½ tablespoon grated lemon zest

¼ teaspoon kosher salt

1 cup plus 5 tablespoons (180g) pastry flour, plus more for shaping

½ cup (1 stick / 115g) cold unsalted butter, cut into ½-inch pieces

1 large egg yolk

1½ tablespoons heavy cream

1 teaspoon vanilla extract

Rum Marshmallow

¾ cup (150g) sugar

3 large egg whites, at room temperature

¼ teaspoon cream of tartar

¼ teaspoon kosher salt

½ teaspoon rum extract

Make the mango pastry cream: In a small bowl, mix together the sugar and egg yolks until well combined. Add the cornstarch, flour, cardamom, and a pinch of salt. Mix well, then set aside; the texture should resemble cookie dough.

In a medium pot over medium heat, whisk together the milk, mango puree, cream, and seeds from the vanilla bean. Bring to a gentle simmer, whisking often, about 5 minutes.

Remove from the heat and ladle about half of the hot milk into the egg mixture, whisking constantly as you add the milk. Transfer the egg mixture to the pot, continuing to whisk constantly, and cook over medium-high heat. Let it come to a rolling boil while whisking, about 3 minutes. Once it comes to a boil, cook further for 30 seconds, until very thick, then remove from the heat.

Whisk in the lime juice and then the butter one piece at a time until fully incorporated, then strain through a fine-mesh sieve into a medium bowl and cover with plastic wrap, placing the plastic directly against the surface of the cream. Refrigerate until cold, about 2 hours. (Pastry cream can be made in advance; transfer to an airtight container and store for up to 2 days.)

Make the pâte sucrée: In a food processor, pulse together the sugar, zest, and salt—you want the zest finely grated. Add the flour and butter and continue to pulse until the mixture resembles breadcrumbs.

In a small bowl, whisk together the egg yolk, cream, and vanilla, then pulse into the dry mixture; the dough will be crumbly but should hold together when pressed between your fingers.

With floured hands, evenly press the crumbly tart dough directly from the food processor into a 9- or 10-inch tart pan. Freeze the crust for 30 minutes. Meanwhile, preheat the oven to 350°F.

Remove the crust from the freezer and dock it by pricking it all over with a fork. Cover the crust with parchment paper and fill the pan with pie weights.

Bake the crust for 25 minutes, then remove the weights and parchment paper and bake until golden brown, another 10 to 12 minutes. Allow to cool on a cooling rack.

Make the rum marshmallow: Fit a stand mixer with the whisk attachment. Fill a medium saucepan with 2 inches of water and place a double boiler or heatproof bowl over the water (making sure it doesn't touch the bowl). Bring the water to a simmer. Add the sugar, egg whites, cream of tartar, and salt to the bowl and heat, whisking continuously, until the sugar has fully dissolved, about 6 minutes.

Transfer the hot egg white mixture to the bowl of the stand mixer. Beat on high until soft peaks form, about 2 minutes, then add the rum extract. Continue to beat until stiff, glossy peaks form, another 5 minutes. Transfer to a piping bag or large zip-top bag and place in the refrigerator. (Marshmallow topping can be made up to 10 days in advance.)

One hour before assembly, remove the pastry cream and marshmallow from the refrigerator.

To assemble the tart, spread the pastry cream into the cooled crust. Snip a hole in the piping bag and fit it with your preferred piping tip (or simply snip a hole). Pipe marshmallow over the pastry cream in any design or pattern. If desired, use a kitchen torch to toast the marshmallow until lightly toasted (or place under the broiler on high, keeping a close eye to avoid burning, 1 to 2 minutes).

Slice and serve immediately.

ATADWE MILK
Tigernut Pudding

Tigernut, a small wrinkly, round nut with a slight sweetness, is an indigenous ingredient to Africa. In Ghanaian cuisine, tigernuts, also known as earth almonds, are used to make drinks, roasted and eaten as a snack, or ground into a flour for baking. Atadwe milk, also known as tigernut pudding, shows off the unique sweetness of this ingredient in a delicious pudding that reminds so many Ghanaians of home. The dessert is adorned with Biscoff cookies for another sweet note that plays off the caramel flavor profile, but feel free to add additional caramel or fresh fruit to the pudding if you'd like. Tigernuts can be sourced in your local Caribbean or Asian market, as well as online.

3 cups (340g) fresh tigernuts

1 cup (195g) jasmine rice

1 cup (200g) sugar

⅓ cup (80g) warm water

1 teaspoon freshly grated nutmeg

½ teaspoon vanilla bean paste or vanilla extract

¼ cup (60g) evaporated milk, plus more to finish

½ teaspoon kosher salt

⅔ cup (75g) crumbled Biscoff cookies, plus more whole cookies for garnish

Shaved chocolate, for garnish (optional)

In a large bowl, rinse the tigernuts to remove impurities. In another large bowl, rinse the rice until the water runs clear. Cover the tigernuts and rice with enough water to fully submerge them. Soak overnight.

The next day to make the caramel, in a medium saucepan over medium-high heat, heat the sugar until it has dissolved, 5 to 7 minutes. Do not stir the sugar during this process but rather swirl the pot around as it melts. If there is any sugar that has built up on the sides of the pan, simply brush it away with a pastry brush dipped in warm water. When the sugar turns an amber color, add the warm water very carefully to the pot and use a wooden spoon to carefully stir. Remove the pan from the heat and set aside to cool completely.

To make the pudding, drain the tigernuts and rice and rinse both once more. Combine the tigernuts and rice in a blender or food processor and pulse to form a coarse flour. Add 3 cups (720g) of water and blend on high to form a smooth puree. Line a large bowl with cheesecloth. Pour the blended mixture in small batches into the cheesecloth and carefully squeeze the liquid into the bowl to extract the milk.

Remove the solids from the cheesecloth and return them to the blender. Add 2 cups (475g) of water, blend again on high, and pour back into the cheesecloth to extract more milk. Discard the solids once completely wrung out. Strain the milk through a fine-mesh sieve.

Pour the strained milk into a large saucepan and add the nutmeg and vanilla paste. Stir to mix evenly and place over medium-low heat. Using a whisk, continuously stir the mixture in the same direction (to prevent clumping) until it starts to thicken, 10 to 15 minutes. Once it has thickened, stir in the evaporated milk.

Recipe continues

Add the caramel, stir, and let simmer until well combined, about 2 minutes. Season with the salt. Remove from the heat and let cool partially. When the pudding is slightly cool, place plastic wrap on the surface to prevent any skin from forming until you're ready to serve.

Serve the pudding warm. Divide half of the crushed cookies evenly among 4 to 6 dessert glasses, then pour the tigernut pudding on top. Pour a splash of evaporated milk on top of the pudding, then garnish with more crumbled cookies and a whole Biscoff cookie in each serving. Top with shaved chocolate, if desired, then serve. The pudding will keep in an airtight container in the refrigerator for up to 7 days. (Place your desired amount of chilled pudding in the microwave for 1 minute before enjoying.)

MALTED BARLEY ICE CREAM

Makes about 4 cups

Grape-Nuts ice cream is a popular dessert in the Caribbean, particularly in countries like Jamaica and Trinidad and Tobago. It's often served as a refreshing treat on hot days. It's close to a classic churned vanilla-based custard but with the addition of brown sugar, which complements the cereal. My memories of eating Grape-Nuts ice cream in New York City are extensive: I remember getting a few scoops while out with my dad some Sunday nights and downing it in milkshake form once I returned from London and was working at the Harlem Children's Zone. Enjoy the ice cream on its own or with fresh fruit, a caramel topping, or with some flaky sea salt.

6 large egg yolks

½ cup (100g) granulated sugar

⅓ cup (75g) (packed) light
   brown sugar

2 cups (475g) heavy cream

1 cup (240g) whole milk

2 teaspoons vanilla bean paste
   or vanilla extract

¼ teaspoon kosher salt

1 cup (110g) Grape-Nuts cereal

In a medium bowl, whisk together the egg yolks, granulated sugar, and brown sugar until light in color and creamy, about 3 minutes.

In a medium saucepan over medium heat, combine the cream and milk. Bring to a simmer, then remove the pan from the heat. While whisking the egg mixture constantly, add a few tablespoons of the hot milk mixture to the egg mixture. Continue to add the milk mixture a few tablespoons at a time until all of the milk mixture has been incorporated.

Pour the egg mixture into the saucepan and cook over medium-low heat, whisking constantly, until the mixture thickens, 3 to 4 minutes. The mixture should coat the back of a spoon and you should be able to draw a clean line across the spoon with your finger. Remove the pan from the heat. Add the vanilla paste and salt and whisk until well combined.

Fill a large bowl with ice. Transfer the custard to a medium bowl and set it inside the bowl of ice. Whisk the custard constantly until cool, about 5 minutes. Cover with plastic wrap, pressing the plastic against the surface of the custard so that it does not form a skin, and refrigerate for at least 8 hours or, ideally, overnight.

Pour the custard in an ice cream machine and churn according to the manufacturer's directions until it has reached a soft-serve consistency. With the machine running, slowly add the Grape-Nuts and continue to churn until fully incorporated.

Serve immediately for soft-serve-style ice cream, or transfer to an airtight container and freeze for at least 4 hours for a firmer ice cream. The ice cream will keep in the freezer for up to 2 weeks.

Acknowledgments

This project started in 2019 and has spanned three continents: Africa, North America, and Europe. There have been so many people who have helped bring this project to life and that means there are so many people to thank.

First, thank you to my mom and dad, who have supported me through this journey. I also want to thank my brothers and sisters, all of my cousins, and my best friends. My friends since childhood (you know who you are): I love you guys.

Lennox, I LOVE YOU! Thank you for being my motivation, baby. I can't wait to share more amazing memories with you.

Jennifer Sit and the team at Clarkson Potter, thank you for your patience and your ability to see our vision for the book, marry it with your own, and still give us room to make mistakes, be curious, and really take this book and make it ours. Jenn, thank you for your transparency during this whole process; I really appreciate you.

To my chef friends and the people I've worked with from my line cook days in New York, Rhode Island, and Washington, D.C., thank you for teaching me work ethic and all of the skills necessary to be good at what I do. Those lessons are imperative to how I think about food right now. Derek Wagner, Eric Ramirez, and Alex Guarnaschelli, thank you for offering feedback.

Shout-out to Cierra Spurlock, my assistant, who keeps me on track.

Thank you to Korsha Wilson for supporting me on this book and saying yes to this project. I really appreciate your seeing this through with me. I would not want this book to come out with anyone else other than you, so I really am grateful for your work and for making me sound all scholarly.

Thank you to Shab Azma, Brooklyn Huang, and the entire team at ARC Collective. Thank you to Ross Yoon Agency and Howard for his help with this book. And thank you to my agents at Verve for being part of this team too.

I owe a lot of gratitude to the folks who helped with capturing these recipes during our cookbook shoot. Thank you to our photographer, Doaa Elkady, and our food stylist, Liberty Fennell. Thank you to Nana Araba Wilmot and Tyrik Smith for all of your culinary help!

Thank you to Carlos Idun-Tawiah for the beautiful photos in Ghana, and to Sena for helping coordinate everything when we were there.

Thank you to Alexander Smalls, BJ Dennis, Carla Hall, Pierre Thiam, and Dr. Jessica B. Harris. Whether it was through personal conversations or through your work or your own writing, you've had a profound impact on me and my work.

And finally a shout-out to the diaspora, the places that inspired this work and continue to teach me: Ghana, New York City, London, the Caribbean, the American South, hip hop, the fashions and foods as well as the music. PEACE!

Index

Published in the United States by Clarkson Potter/Publishers, an imprint of the Crown Publishing
Group, a division of Penguin Random House LLC, New York.
clarksonpotter.com

CLARKSON POTTER is a trademark and POTTER with colophon is a registered trademark of
Penguin Random House LLC.

Library of Congress Cataloging-in-Publication Data
Names: Adjepong, Eric, author. | Wilson, Korsha, author. | Elkady, Doaa, photographer. | Idun-
Tawiah, Carlos, photographer. Title: Ghana to the World / Eric Adjepong with Korsha Wilson ;
photographs by Doaa Elkady and Carlos Idun-Tawiah. Description: New York : Clarkson Potter/
Publishers, [2025] | Includes index. Identifiers: LCCN 2023052323 (print) | LCCN 2023052324
(ebook) | ISBN 9780593234778 (hardcover) | ISBN 9780593234785 (e-pub) Subjects: LCSH:
Cooking, Ghanaian. | Cooking, West African. | LCGFT: Cookbooks. Classification: LCC TX725.G4
A29 2025 (print) | LCC TX725.G4 (ebook) | DDC 641.59667--dc23/eng/20240228
LC record available at https://lccn.loc.gov/2023052323
LC ebook record available at https://lccn.loc.gov/2023052324

ISBN 978-0-593-23477-8
Ebook ISBN 978-0-593-23478-5

Printed in China

Editor: Jennifer Sit
Editorial assistant: Elaine Hennig
Designer: Ian Dingman
Illustrator: Chelsea Charles
Production editor: Sohayla Farman
Production manager: Phil Leung
Compositors: Merri Ann Morrell and Hannah Hunt
Food stylist: Liberty Fennell
Food stylist assistants: Nana Araba Wilmot, Aaron Meftah, and Tyrik Smith
Prop stylist: Alya Hameedi
Photo assistant: Angela Cholmondeley
Copyeditor: Amy Kovalski
Proofreaders: Rachel Markowitz and Heather Rodino
Indexer: Ken DellaPenta
Publicist: Jina Stanfill
Marketer: Monica Stanton

10 9 8 7 6 5 4 3 2 1

First Edition